Chambers
card tricks

great tricks to amaze and amuse

Peter Eldin
member of The Magic Circle

Chambers

CHAMBERS
An imprint of Chambers Harrap Publishers Ltd
7 Hopetoun Crescent, Edinburgh, EH7 4AY

Chambers Harrap is an Hachette UK company

© Peter Eldin under licence to Chambers Harrap Publishers Limited 2009

Chambers® is a registered trademark of Chambers Harrap Publishers Ltd

First published by Chambers Harrap Publishers Ltd 2009

A CIP catalogue record for this book is available from the British Library.

ISBN 978 0550 10471 7

10 9 8 7 6 5 4 3 2 1

www.chambers.co.uk

Designed by Chambers Harrap Publishers Ltd, Edinburgh
Typeset in Serifa by raspberryhmac graphic design and typesetting services
Hand illustrations: Richard Duszczak
Other illustrations: Heather Macpherson
Printed and bound in Spain by Graphy Cems

Contributors

Author
Peter Eldin

Chambers Editor
Anne Robertson

Editorial Assistance
Katharine Coates

Prepress
Nico Echallier
Heather Macpherson
Becky Pickard

Illustrations
Richard Duszczak
Nico Echallier
Heather Macpherson

Publishing Manager
Hazel Norris

Editorial Director
Vivian Marr

About the author

Peter Eldin has studied conjuring since he was nine, when he became a member of the Boy Magicians' Club, the starting point for many professional magicians. Later he joined The London Society of Magicians, The Luton Mystic Ring, The Watford Association of Magicians, The International Brotherhood of Magicians, The Society of American Magicians and The Magic Circle, the world's most prestigious magic club.

Peter has performed magic all over Britain and has been the subject of numerous media interviews in the UK and America. For eight years he was editor of *The Magic Circular*, the magazine of The Magic Circle. He has also edited *Abracadabra*, the world's only magical weekly. He has authored several internationally successful books on magic and many other subjects, as well as providing material for periodicals, radio and television.

Contents

Contents

Index

Introduction by Peter Eldin

Card tricks account for the greater proportion of tricks popular with magicians. Partly this is because there are no props to carry, everyone is familiar with a pack of cards and there are an infinite number of tricks that can be performed. A pack of cards is easily carried and most people have at least one pack in the house. Also card tricks can be performed in any setting: in a private house, a pub, a restaurant, on a train or even in the street.

Another attraction of card tricks is that they can be performed impromptu (or apparently so, for they must be practised and rehearsed first). It is particularly impressive if someone hands you a pack of cards with the request 'show us a trick' and you can entertain them.

With just a pack of cards and your own personality you can bring magic and entertainment to audiences of all ages, races and creeds. You do not need expensive apparatus to become a competent and much appreciated performer. With a pack of cards and a likable personality, the world is your oyster!

In this book the tricks are arranged alphabetically to make it easy to refer back to a trick at any time. If you are new to card magic, it is recommended that you learn some of the easy tricks first. Each trick is labelled with a skill level to enable you to pick these out. Although the tricks have been categorized as easy, moderate or advanced there is really nothing difficult in any of the tricks.

Some of the tricks make use of magic techniques such as special shuffles and cuts. You will find illustrated instructions for these techniques on ppix–xxv. In the introductory panel of each trick, it is made explicit which techniques are required under the heading 'Special techniques'.

Each of the tricks has been allocated a category to indicate the type of trick it is. Many card tricks are of the 'location' kind – a spectator chooses or takes a card and the performer then finds or identifies it after it has been returned to the pack. It is a wise performer who does not include too many of these tricks in one showing, although they can be made entertaining by the varying means by which the card is found. When performing an act or sequence of card tricks, however, you should endeavour to include some other types of card tricks.

Other tricks are categorized as mind-reading, skill demonstration, transformation and transposition. 'Mind-reading' covers any tricks in which the performer appears to possess amazing mental abilities to read minds or transfer thoughts to others. 'Skill demonstration' describes tricks in which the performer appears to show great technical skill in handling the cards. 'Transformation' is used for tricks in which things (in this case, cards) appear to change from one thing to another and 'transposition' means the mysterious movement of a card or cards to another location. There is one trick in this book which does not follow these types and that is Ditto (see p25) which is labelled 'coincidence'. This is simply because that is what it appears to be – a coincidence!

You will notice that in this book the performer is always masculine. This is not meant to be sexist in any way for there are many excellent female magicians, it is just a way of avoiding using 'he or she' or even 's/he' in the descriptions.

There are several types of playing cards but the two most popular sizes are bridge size (56 x 87mm) and poker size (63 x 88mm). Cheap packs of cards are produced on thin board and will not last very long whereas better quality cards will last for a long time and will be easier to use. Always use the best cards that you can afford and do not use them for anything other than magic. Using your cards for games will make them harder to use for tricks as they will become sticky and grubby.

Virtually every book on conjuring includes the three basic rules for success – practise, practise and practise again. Whilst it is true that practice makes perfect there is no need to make heavy work of it. Practising moves need not be a chore for they can be done whilst relaxing in front of the television or even reading a book! This is actually an advantage for it means that you are not looking at your hands. Many performers give the game away by watching their hands as they make a crucial move. Don't look at your hands; look at your audience. Even the simplest of tricks should be practised until you can do it without concentrating on the methodology. You should also practise how you are going to stand or sit in front of your audience and know what you are going to say at any point.

Please do not just read how a trick is done and then immediately show it to someone. Some aspects of card tricks may be a little confusing when you read them so you should always read with a pack of cards handy so you can follow the trick with the cards in your hands. When you understand the method and the effect of a trick try it out in private several times before showing it to anyone. Never accept a trick as a finished product. Try to add to it in some way by injecting it with your own personality, drawing in the audience as part of the magical experience and, if need be, changing it completely. After a while the tricks will no longer be just tricks, they will be part of your persona.

There are a hundred tricks in this book. This does not mean that you should bore your audience with all of them at once. Keep your performances restricted to no more than five tricks at most. Your job as a performer is not to show how clever you are at doing card tricks. Your job is to entertain your audience, not to bore them, and it is not entertaining to show everything you know.

Above all, please enjoy your magic. If you do not enjoy it then neither will your audience.

Peter Eldin

Basic Techniques

There are literally hundreds of basic techniques, or 'sleights', in card magic and new ones are being devised all the time. You do not need to know many of these to put on a show of entertaining card tricks but you should, however, learn at least some of them for they are, to a performer of magic tricks, like musical scales to a musician. They are the building blocks that you can use to achieve amazing effects, and you must practise them until you can do them perfectly. This need not be hard work, though, as you can do them while you are, for example, watching television. The key thing about these basics is that, thanks to all your practice, the audience should not be aware that they are taking place. The art of this art is concealing the art!

It is often said that 'the hand is quicker than the eye'. In fact, nothing is further from the truth, for any quick or erratic movements will attract the audience's attention. Even though your spectators may not know exactly what you have done, they will be aware that you have done something to mislead them. All your movements should be unhurried and carried out at a normal pace, so remember to take your time when performing.

This book is written as if the performer is right-handed but this is a matter of convenience. If you are left-handed you may have to change the position of your hands to do the trick. The author is right-handed but he always uses his left hand to perform the Charlier Cut (see pxvi). Throughout the book all the deals and card spreads are described as going from left to right so if you normally work from right to left you may have to give the presentation of material a little more thought.

People's hands and abilities are different so if you are not comfortable with a certain technique there is nothing to stop you changing it to suit yourself, provided that it remains deceptive and that the audience do not know what you are doing.

I would suggest that you learn the techniques as and when you come across a trick that needs one of them. Where a trick requires a special technique, there is a cross-reference in the text so that you can quickly find out all about it. Sometimes, when you are practising a trick or a move for the first few times, you may find that the cards fly out of your hands. This can be very frustrating, but do not give up – you will get there eventually. It is actually a good idea to do your initial practising while you are sitting on a bed: this makes it a whole lot easier to recover the cards when you drop them!

Magic Words
Conjuring, like a lot of professions, makes use of words which mean something specific to others in the business. Every effort has been made to avoid these special words but a few still require a little explanation.

A 'pack' means a complete set of 52 playing cards (another name for a pack, frequently used by magicians, is 'deck'). A pack is usually contained in a cardboard box but it is also possible to buy fancy boxes to make your performance more showy. Where reference is made to a 'packet' this means a group of cards squared up, and 'squaring' the cards means pushing the cards in the pack or packet together neatly. Another word is 'pile' and this is used to describe a group of cards dealt onto the table.

Several tricks require the use of a 'stacked pack'. This is a pack in which all of the cards in the pack are in a prearranged, memorized order. Only one, Eight Kings sequence (see pxix), is given in this book but there are many others used by magicians. Sometimes just a few cards are arranged in a special order before the performance of a trick and this is generally referred to as a 'set-up'.

For a few of the tricks in this book you will need a 'confederate' – someone who secretly helps the performer do the trick. The audience must not realize that this person is part of the secret of the trick.

The words used for the parts of a playing card can be seen in the illustration below.

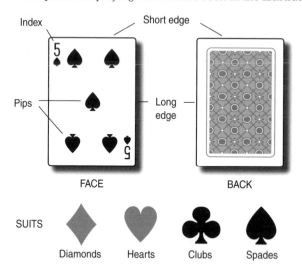

Throughout the book there are lots of details about the positioning of various fingers. The illustration below will help you know which finger is being described.

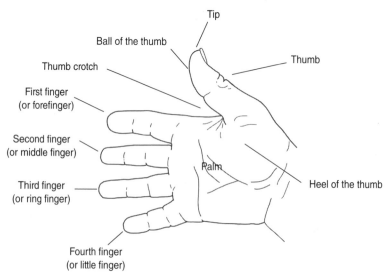

Shuffles

Overhand Shuffle

This is a standard shuffle used by card players all over the world. Hold the pack in your left hand, with the cards resting on your middle, ring and little fingers. Your thumb should be against the back of the top card and your forefinger should be at the narrow end of the pack furthest from your body in order to keep the cards aligned.

Bring your right hand to the pack and lift out most of the lower part of the pack. Bring these cards over the cards remaining in your left hand, allowing a few cards to fall from those in your right hand on top of those in your left hand as you do so. Lift your right hand and repeat, once again allowing some cards to fall from your right hand into your left. Keep doing this until all the cards from your right hand have been shuffled onto those in your left hand. Repeat all these actions two or three more times to complete the shuffle.

Riffle Shuffle

This is another standard shuffle used by card players. Divide the pack into two, and take one half in your left hand and the other in your right hand. Then interlace the two halves of the pack together as follows. Your thumb should be on the centre of the short edge nearest you and your middle and ring fingers on the opposite short side. Your forefinger should be bent over on top of the cards and your little finger should be against the long side nearest your body (see illustration 1 below).

①

Bring the two halves of the pack together and allow the cards to fall from your right and left thumbs alternately (these do not have to be single cards until you become an expert). When all the cards have fallen, push the two halves together, squaring them up as you do so, and the shuffle is complete (see illustration 2 below).

②

Weave Shuffle

Hold the pack in your left hand. Lift off the top half of the pack with your right hand and then tap together the two ends of each half-pack, to make sure that the ends of the two halves are perfectly square (see illustration 1 below).

①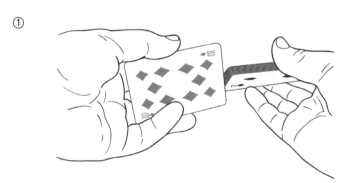

Press the two corners nearest you into one another so that the cards begin to weave together – a slight movement back and forth may make this easier to do – and then push the two halves completely together so that the pack is completely reassembled (see illustration 2 below).

②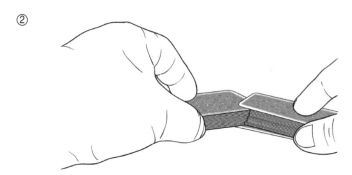

False Shuffles

There are many ways to shuffle a pack of cards and yet retain certain cards in the same position as they were at the start. These shuffles are known to magicians as 'false shuffles'.

Single Card Shuffle

In many tricks a card that has been selected by a spectator is returned, face down, to the top of the pack. To move the card secretly from the top to the bottom of the pack, start an overhand shuffle by using your right hand to lift out all the cards with the exception of the top card. Now shuffle the cards from your right hand in the normal way. When the shuffle is complete, the selected card is at the bottom of the pack.

To move a card secretly from the bottom to the top of the pack, you perform a normal overhand shuffle and keep shuffling until you have just one card in your right hand. You then drop that single card – the card from the bottom of the pack – on top of the pack, to complete the shuffle.

If you want to keep the bottom card at the bottom of the pack, lift off two-thirds of the pack in the normal way, with the exception of the bottom card, which is held back by pressure from your left fingers. Then shuffle the cards in the usual way, retaining the bottom card on the bottom of the pack.

Injog False Shuffle
This is a method for keeping one card – or several cards – on the top of the pack. Hold the cards in your left hand ready for an overhand shuffle. With your right hand, take a packet of cards from the bottom of the pack, making sure that you cut the pack below the cards you wish to keep on top. Shuffle off one card from the top of the cards in your right hand onto those in your left hand, but move it slightly towards your body before you drop it so that the card protrudes over the end of the packet in your left hand (see illustration below).

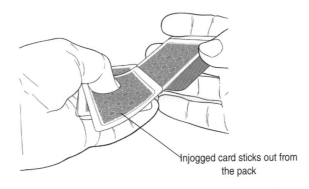

Injogged card sticks out from
the pack

Now shuffle off the rest of the cards using a normal overhand shuffle. You will now have one card sticking out from the rest of the pack (magicians call this an 'injog'). The easiest way to continue is to bring your right hand up beneath the cards until your right thumb hits the injogged card. Push it upwards a little so that you can grasp all the cards beneath this card using your right fingers. Then use your right thumbnail to push the injogged card flush with the rest of the pack as you take the cards below the injogged card with your right fingers and place them on the top of the pack. This will bring the card, or cards, you wish to retain back on top of the pack.

This technique is over 400 years old but is still a major part of card magic to this day. When you first try this, injog the card about 2cm and shuffle the cards irregularly on top in order to conceal the protruding card. With practice you should be able to reduce the amount of injog so that the cards can be shuffled more neatly.

Forces
In many tricks you have to ensure that a spectator takes the card you want him to take, although you appear to be giving him a free choice. Magicians call this 'forcing' and there are literally hundreds of different ways of achieving this, a few of which are described here.

Cross Cut Force
The card you want to force has to be on the top of the pack at the start of the trick. Give the pack a false shuffle (see pxii), retaining the top card on top of the pack, and place the pack on the table. Ask a spectator to lift off some of the cards and place them on the table to the

right. Then pick up the rest of the cards and place them on top of the cards that have just been cut, but at a 90° angle, 'to mark the cut' (see illustration below).

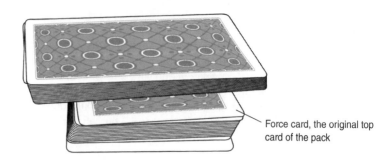

Force card, the original top card of the pack

You then have to talk for a while to allow the audience to forget exactly what has taken place. Next lift off the top half of the pack and point to the top card of the bottom half as you say 'Will you please take a look at the card you have cut to, but do not let me see it.' It appears that the spectator has had a perfectly free choice because he cut the cards himself but he has, in fact, taken what was originally the top card of the pack and you can now proceed with the rest of your performance knowing which card the spectator has taken.

This force sounds too simple to be effective and yet it is very popular with magicians. Try it out a few times and see how convincing it is.

Reverse Force
For this force you need to know the top card of the pack. False shuffle (see pxii) the pack, retaining the top card on top of the pack. Hold the pack, face down, in your left hand as you ask a spectator to lift off any number of cards. Then turn the cut-off portion face up and put it back on top of the cards in your hand, 'to mark the cut'.

Take the pack in your right hand and turn it over as you ribbon spread (see pxix) the cards on the table. Push out the first face-down card you come to – the point where the face-up and face-down cards meet – and ask the spectator to look at it and remember it. The card the spectator is looking at is the forced card, the original top card of the pack.

Running Force
The card to be forced is on top of the pack. Hold the pack in your left hand and count the top few cards into your right hand. Push over more cards on top of those in your left hand until a spectator calls 'Stop!' (see illustration below).

The force card, the original top card of the pack

View from below

Then cut the pack at that point and show the force card, which is now at the bottom of those in your right hand, to the spectator.

Cuts

Hand Cut

Hold the pack in your left hand. With your right hand, lift off about half of the pack. Now take the cards remaining in your left hand (the original bottom half of the pack) and place them on top of the cards in your right. This is known as 'cutting the cards and completing the cut'.

Tabled Cut

Place the pack on the table. Using your right hand, lift off about half of the cards and place them on the table to the right. Now pick up what was the bottom half of the pack and put these cards on top of what was the top half, to complete the cut.

Swing Cut

This is a pleasing, professional-looking method for cutting a pack of cards. Hold the pack in your right hand from above, move your right forefinger to the left corner of the pack (which is furthest away from your body) and, with the tip of this finger, lift up some of the cards.

Holding this top portion between your right thumb and forefinger, move your forefinger to the left and deposit the cards in the crotch of your left thumb (see illustrations 1 and 2 below).

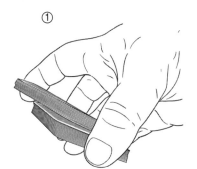
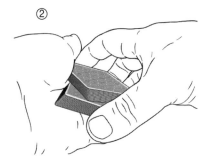

Now bring your right hand over to your left and drop the original bottom cards on top of those in your left hand.

Swivel Cut

This is another pleasing way to cut a pack of cards. Start off by holding the pack in your right hand from above, with your right thumb beneath the short end of the pack nearer you, and then bring your left forefinger up to the bottom-left corner of the pack (to the left of your right thumb), with the middle finger of your right hand against the far short edge of the pack.

Now push the top half of the pack away from you, using the middle finger of your right hand as a pivot (see illustration overleaf).

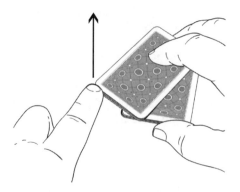

Continue this movement and gradually turn your left hand palm upwards until the cards on the top half of the pack drop onto your left palm. To finish the cut, drop the cards from your right hand on top of those in your left.

Charlier Cut

This amusing way to cut a pack of cards is named after Charlier, a French card magician about whom very little is known (although it is believed that he was more of a card sharp than a magician). Although it is used by magicians as a flourish (a showy demonstration of the performer's skill), it can be used to great effect in certain card tricks.

Hold the pack in your right hand with your thumb on the long edge closest to you, your middle and ring fingers on the opposite long edge and your forefinger and little finger on each of the short ends. Drop about half of the cards from your thumb so that they fall onto your fingers and palm (see illustration 1 below).

①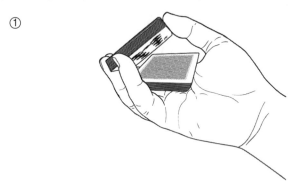

Now move your forefinger so that it comes into contact with the bottom card of the lower portion. Using your forefinger, push the lower portion towards your thumb (see illustration 2 opposite).

When the cards touch your thumb, allow them to fall over and on top of the top half of the pack, then bring your forefinger back to its original position, as your left hand comes over to square up the cards (see illustration 3 below).

 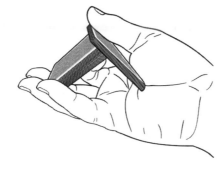

To help prevent the cards from falling, use your little finger to keep the pack square at the end. Do not worry if you drop cards while you are practising – just pick them up and try again.

When you can perform this cut with your right hand, try it with your left and, for practice, try doing it with two packs simultaneously, holding one pack in each hand!

False Cuts
As the name implies, a false cut is a method of apparently giving the cards a genuine cut but, in reality, keeping the whole pack in the same order.

Simple False Cut
This is one of those moves that do not sound convincing when you read about them. However, the method really is very effective, so please do try it out.

Hold the pack in your left hand with your thumb on the left-hand long side, your forefinger resting against the bottom far-right corner of the pack and your other three fingers on the right-hand long side. Use your right thumb and forefinger to pull out about half of the cards from the bottom of the pack. Then bring your right hand towards your body and back over your left hand, to place the cards on the table. As your right hand passes over your left, allow the cards in your left hand to drop down onto your left palm.

Now bring your right hand back to join your left hand, in order to take the rest of the cards and place them on top of the cards on the table.

It appears that the pack has been genuinely cut into two halves and then reassembled but the cards are, in fact, in exactly the same order as they were at the start.

Triple False Cut
Visualize the pack as if it were divided into three sections. Hold the pack in your left hand, with the back of your hand uppermost and, with your right hand, pull out the centre third of the pack (section B: see illustration 1 below) and place it on the table in front of you.

①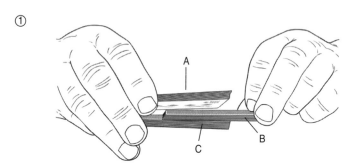

Now drop the bottom third of the pack (section C) in front of the cards on the table and the top portion (section A) in front of that (see illustration 2 below).

②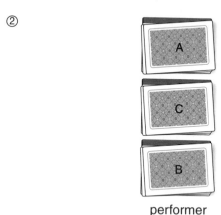

performer

With your right hand, pick up the pile furthest from you (section A) and put it in your left hand. Now pick up the cards that formed the centre pile (section C) and place them on top of the cards in your left hand, but keeping the little finger of your left hand between the two sets of cards. Finally, pick up the cards nearest you (section B) and place them on top of the cards in your left hand. Lift off all the cards above your left little finger and place them beneath the cards in your left hand. It appears that the cards have been well mixed by this sequence of cuts but in fact they are in exactly the same order as when you started!

Spreads

Hand to Hand

This is the move most commonly used to allow a spectator to choose a card from the pack. Hold the cards in your left hand as if you were about to start dealing them and use your left thumb to push cards from the top to the right and into the crotch of your right thumb. Then use your left thumb to push more cards to the right underneath those already in your right hand. Continue pushing cards over, supporting them from below using the fingers of both hands until you have a nice, uniform spread of cards. To close up the spread, simply bring your hands together until all the cards are back in your left hand. This spread can also be used with the cards face up for certain tricks.

Ribbon Spread

The ribbon spread is a simple display of cards on the table. Hold the pack in your right hand, bring your hand down onto the table towards your left side and then move your forefinger so that it rests against the left long edge of the pack. Move the cards to your right in a straight line as you allow them to slide from the bottom and onto the table (see illustration below).

You must move your hand smoothly as your right forefinger determines the distance between each card as it spreads from the bottom. Keep going until all the cards are on the table in an even spread. Although it appears to be simple, it can take quite a bit of practice to get it perfect every time. However, the result is well worth the effort. You will also find that it works best using good-quality cards and with a thick cloth on the table.

Miscellaneous Techniques

Stacked Pack

There are various methods of keeping the pack in a set order. One of these is known as the Eight Kings sequence. To memorize the sequence, you have to learn a little rhyme: eight kings threatened to save ninety-five ladies for one sick knave. The card values associated with the words of the rhyme are as follows: eight (8) kings (K) threatened (3, 10) to (2) save (7) ninety-five (9, 5) ladies (Q) for (4) one (A) sick (6) knave (J). The suits of the cards are also in a set order – Clubs, Hearts, Spades, Diamonds – which you can remember using the mnemonic CHaSeD.

To set up the stack, first divide the pack into the four suits. Take 8♣, place it face up on the table, put K♥ on top and follow with 3♠, 10♦, 2♣, 7♥, 9♠, 5♦, Q♣, 4♥, A♠, 6♦, J♣ and continue stacking the pack in this manner until all the cards have been used.

With the pack stacked in this sequence you can always tell which card has been taken just by looking at the card above it. The easiest way to do this is to cut the cards at the point from which the card was taken and then look at the bottom card of the pack. If, for example, the bottom card is 9♦, you know that the removed card must be 5♣, and so on. If the card that was removed is then returned to the top or the bottom of the pack, the cyclical arrangement is restored.

The pack can also be cut several times without destroying the arrangement.

Glide

The glide is a way of keeping a particular card on the bottom of the pack by apparently withdrawing cards from the bottom, but in fact removing the card second from the bottom of the pack. Hold the pack in your left hand with the back of your hand uppermost, your forefinger and little finger at the long edge and your middle and ring fingers touching the face of the bottom card. Use the tip of your middle and ring fingers to push the bottom card back about 1cm. You will have to move your little finger away from the cards to do this (see illustration below).

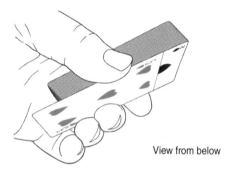

View from below

Using your right fingers, take the bottom card from the pack. However, as the bottom card is indented, your fingers will come into contact with the card second from bottom which you pull out face down.

As soon as you want to withdraw the real bottom card, you simply push your right fingers further inward and then pull out the real bottom card.

Double Lift

This is a method for apparently showing the top card in a pack but actually showing the card second from the top. Although this is in essence a very straightforward move, magicians have devised many different techniques for achieving it. The following is a very simple method.

Hold the pack face down in your left hand. Now bring your right hand to the pack with your forefinger and middle finger at the front of the pack and your thumb to the rear. Press your right fingers back towards you a little, causing the top few cards to move back slightly. This makes it easier for you then to use the ball of your thumb to lift up the two top cards together (see illustration 1 opposite).

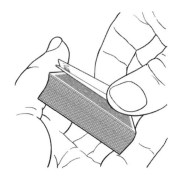

At this point you can lift off the two top cards as one. However, it is usually better practice to use the tip of your left little finger to hold them apart from the rest of the pack to create a break and your right hand can be withdrawn (see illustration 2 below).

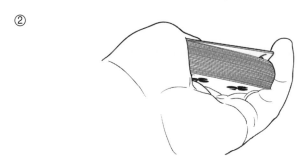

After a few seconds (or more if need be), return your right hand to the pack, lift off the two cards as one and place them, face up, on the top of the pack (see illustration 3 below).

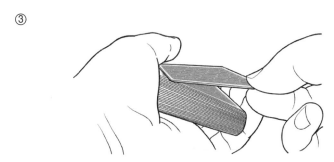

It is a good idea to place them sitting slightly over the edge of the pack as this makes it easier to lift them up again and place them back face down on the top of the pack. To the audience it should appear that you have simply turned the top card face up and then turned it face down again. You can then deal off the top card for a particular trick but this will not, of course, be the card the audience think it is.

The real secret of the double lift is that it should appear natural and above suspicion. Magicians have perfected many different techniques to make this move natural.

Break Control

For many card tricks it is necessary to bring a card to the top of the pack. There are several ways to do this but this break control is one of the easiest. Fan out the cards and invite a spectator to take one of them. Then lift off about half of the pack and ask the spectator to replace his card on the lower half. Put the upper half of the pack back on top of the chosen card, but secretly put the tip of your little finger on top of the replaced card before replacing the top half of the pack. Now lift off about a quarter of the pack and place it on the table, quickly followed by the second quarter or so (be sure to cut the cards above the break, ie above your little finger) and place them on top of the cards on the table. Finally place the remaining cards in your hand onto those on the table. It will appear to the audience that the chosen card is now lost somewhere in the pack but it is actually on the top of the pack and ready for you to use.

Palm

The palm is a method of concealing a card (or, indeed, some other object) in the hand. To palm off a card from the top of the pack, hold the pack in your left hand with one of the short ends facing the audience. Now bring your right hand over the pack, ostensibly to square up the cards. With the tip of your right little finger pressing against the top right-hand corner of the pack, push the top card forward just a little, and press down at the same time. This will cause the top card to swivel up into your right hand where it is held in position by the tip of your little finger and the heel of your right thumb (see illustrations 1 and 2 below).

① 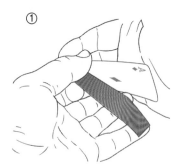 ②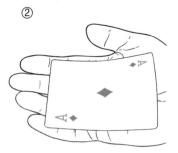

Now move the forefinger, middle and ring fingers of your right hand to the right to square up the pack. From this position you can either place the pack on the table, or hand it to a spectator for shuffling, with the top card remaining hidden in your right hand.

After the pack has been shuffled, take it from the spectator in your left hand and bring your right hand over the top of the cards to square them up, at the same time dropping the palmed card back on top of the pack.

In all of the above moves – as with all sleight of hand – you should be looking at the audience or at the spectator to whom you are talking, and not at your hands. If you look at your hands, the audience will follow your gaze and will soon cotton on to what you are doing.

Glimpse

In many card tricks you will need to know the identity of the top or bottom card of the pack. The easiest way to find this out is to take the pack in your left hand and use your right hand to square up the cards. While you are doing this it is quite easy to tip your right fingers forward until you can see the index of the bottom card at the end of the pack nearer you. You need only the quickest glance to see this, so do not hold this position for too long nor make it obvious that you are looking (see illustration below).

If you need to know the top card of the pack, glimpse the bottom card and then simply do a quick shuffle to bring the bottom card to the top (see pxii).

You will often find that when a spectator shuffles the pack he will inadvertently allow you to see the bottom card. If this happens, make the most of it and, if need be, abandon the trick you had planned to do which does not require knowledge of the bottom card to another trick that does. A good magician makes the most of any opportunities that may occur during a performance.

Crimp

A crimp is simply a bend put in one corner of a playing card. With the pack held in your right hand, bring your left thumb up to the bottom of the pack and push the corner of the bottom card until it bends slightly (see illustration 1 below).

①

Right thumb bends corner of bottom card

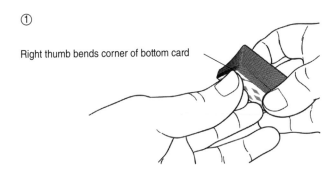

When the pack is cut, the crimp will cause a gap (break) in the pack (see illustration 2 overleaf). This makes it very easy to cut to this card any time you want to position it on the bottom of the pack.

②

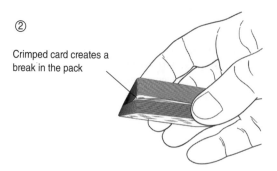

Crimped card creates a
break in the pack

The crimp is very useful when a card has been chosen and returned to the top of the pack. This is because the pack can be cut several times and, when you then cut off all the cards above the break, the chosen card will always be back on top of the pack.

Short Card

As its name suggests, a short card is a card that is a little shorter than all the other cards in the pack. To make a short card, first draw a faint pencil line along both short ends of a playing card (see illustration below).

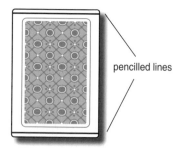

pencilled lines

Use a Joker to practise with. With a sharp pair of scissors, cut carefully along the pencil lines. Now use the scissors to round off the four corners of the card.

Place the short card anywhere in the pack. Hold the cards as if you were about to start dealing them in your left hand. Then bring your right hand over the top of the pack with your forefinger on top of the pack, your right thumb against the end of the pack nearer your body and your middle and ring fingers against the opposite end of the pack. Your right little finger goes against the side of the pack. Using your right thumb, riffle the ends of the cards until you hear a snapping sound. Stop at this sound (which has been made by the short card), cut the cards at that point and the short card will be on the top of the pack.

A simple use of the short card is when you need to ask a spectator to handle the pack but still want to control the position of a particular card. Take the pack back from the spectator and cut the cards, cutting to the short card. Spread the cards, face down, between your hands and have one card chosen and shown to the audience. Ask the spectator to place the chosen card on top of the pack (and on top of the short card) and then cut the pack several times. At any time you like, you can cut the short card to the top of the pack and the chosen card will be on the bottom of the pack.

Secret Reversal

This is a neat way of secretly turning a card face up in the pack while you are holding the cards in full view. Hold the pack in your right hand from above, with the card you wish to reverse on top of the pack. Use the ball of your right thumb to lift the card a little, in this way creating a break beneath it. With your left hand, take the bottom half of the pack, turn it face up and place it on top of the cards in your right hand, continuing to mark the break with your thumb (see illustration 1 below).

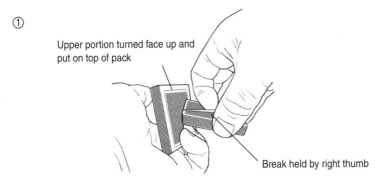

①

Upper portion turned face up and put on top of pack

Break held by right thumb

Now take all the cards below the break, turn them face up and replace them on the bottom of the pack (see illustration 2 below).

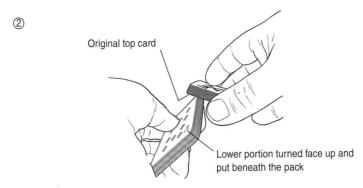

②

Original top card

Lower portion turned face up and put beneath the pack

In this way, the whole pack has been turned over with the exception of the original top card.

To draw attention away from this subtle move (which is known to magicians as the Braue Reversal after its inventor, Frederick Braue), give the pack two more cuts, being very careful not to let the audience see the reversed card. Ribbon spread (see pxix) the cards face up and there will be one card face down in the pack – the original top card (see illustration below).

The face-down card

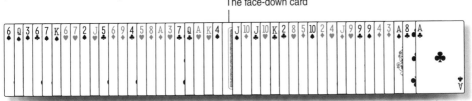

Card Tricks

About Face

The audience are shown two small groups of cards which are then mixed up, face up and face down, by the performer. The cards are shuffled, and are held briefly behind the performer's back. The cards are then brought forward as two packets, and it is seen that they have been arranged so that each packet has exactly the same number of face-up cards. The trick is repeated immediately, as a demonstration of the performer's amazing prowess with the cards.

Type	Skill demonstration
Skill level	Easy
Special techniques	None
Equipment	Pack of cards

Performance

Hold the pack face down in your left hand and push ten cards from the top of the pack into your right hand. Put the little finger of your right hand under these cards, and then push off another ten cards beneath your little finger. Try not to make it obvious that you are counting off a particular number of cards. Put the pack to one side and split the cards you are holding into two packets (the 'break', caused by your little finger, makes this easy to do), one in your right hand and one in your left. Turn the cards in your right hand face up and mix them into the cards in your left hand, so that some of the cards in the packet are face up and some are face down. You can allow a spectator to shuffle the packet of cards if you wish.

Then, holding the cards behind your back, silently count off ten cards into your right hand, turn the right-hand packet over, and then bring both packets to the front. Spread the right packet out on the table and point out how many cards are face up. Spread out the cards in your left hand and exactly the same number of cards are face up!

Pick up the right-hand group of cards and turn them over, before putting them on top of those in your left hand. You can now shuffle the cards (or get a spectator to shuffle them) and repeat the trick.

Tips

This trick works with any number of cards, provided there is the same number in each packet. However, using too many cards would make the trick cumbersome and tedious.

As a general rule, it is bad practice to repeat a trick immediately after performing it but in this case one repeat actually adds to the impact.

Abracadabra

The performer's amazing ability to read minds is demonstrated when he produces the very card chosen by a spectator.

Type	Mind-reading
Skill level	Easy
Special techniques	None
Equipment	Pack of cards

Preparation
Put two cards from the pack you are going to use into one of your pockets.

Performance
Place any three cards from the pack face up on the table and ask a spectator to concentrate on any one of them. You must memorize the three cards and the order they are in. Place the three cards in your pocket, alongside the two hidden cards you placed there earlier. Pretend to concentrate very hard, then take out one of the hidden cards and (without showing its face) place it, face down, on the pack saying to the spectator 'I don't think you are thinking of this one.' Pretend to concentrate hard again and take out the second hidden card and place that, face down, on the pack, also without showing it, as you say 'And I don't think it was this one either.' You still have the three cards taken from the pack earlier in your pocket but the audience believe there is just one card remaining there. Ask the spectator the name of the card he is thinking of and then take that card from your pocket.

Tips
At the end of this trick you are, of course, left with two cards in your pocket, and these will have to be returned to the pack at some point. Take your time over this – there is no hurry – and replace the cards when you can do so without anyone noticing.

Ace Assembly

The pack is divided into four piles and then mixed up, by a spectator, following the performer's instructions. Astoundingly, the top card of each pile is shown to be an Ace.

Type	Location
Skill level	Easy
Special techniques	None
Equipment	Pack of cards

Preparation
Before your performance secretly put the four Aces on top of the pack.

Performance
Place the pack, face down, on the table and ask a spectator to pick it up and to divide it, working from the bottom of the pack, into four roughly equal piles of cards, which he is to set out in a row. Keep track of the top part of the pack containing the Aces: this will end up at either the left-hand or right-hand end of the row of piles, depending on the way in which the spectator has placed the cards. Point to the pile at the opposite end to the one containing the Aces and ask the spectator to pick it up, take three cards from the top of the pile and place them on the bottom and then to deal one card from the top of that pile onto each of the other three piles. Then you ask the spectator to repeat the same procedure with the other piles in the row, taking the three cards from the top to the bottom of each pile, and then dealing one card from the top of the pile on to each of the other three piles. When the spectator has done this for all four piles, pause for a moment to allow the audience to take in what has happened. Then ask the spectator to turn over the top card of each pile – they are the four Aces!

Tips
As you do not touch the cards during the trick, you can pretend that you are exerting some magical force over the Aces to bring one to the top of each pile. It is also more impressive if, at the start of the trick, you give the cards a false shuffle (see pxii), retaining the Aces at the top of the pack.

Ace Detective

A pack of cards is shuffled and is held by the performer behind his back. The performer's ultra-sensitive fingertips and power over the cards are then used to produce the four Aces from the pack.

Type	Skill demonstration
Skill level	Easy
Special techniques	None
Equipment	Pack of cards, safety pin, paper clip

Preparation

Take the four Aces from the pack and place them in the paper clip. Then slip the paper clip onto the safety pin, and attach the pin securely to the lining of your jacket at the rear making sure that the Aces do not hang down below the hem of your jacket (see illustration below).

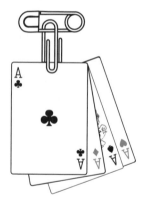

Performance

Ask a member of the audience to shuffle the remaining cards and then fan them out, face up, between your hands to show that they are well mixed. Immediately, close up the fan, square up the cards and tell the audience that you will now employ your amazing dexterity and affinity with the cards to locate the four Aces. To make the feat even more impressive you will find the four Aces with the cards held behind your back.

Holding the pack of cards behind your back, secretly pull the four Aces from the hidden clip. Take one of the Aces and place it face up on the table, and then bring forward the remaining three, one by one, as you pretend to locate them in the shuffled pack.

Tips
The safety pin and clip (magicians call a hidden aid such as this 'a gimmick') can also be used to add a few cards secretly to the top of a pack should you need them for a particular trick.

Ace to Ten

A small packet of cards is taken and is used to spell out the numbers from one to ten, with one card being moved from the top to the bottom of the packet for each letter. The card of the matching value is turned up after each number is spelled out.

Type	Skill demonstration
Skill level	Easy
Special techniques	None
Equipment	Pack of cards

Preparation
Put ten cards (the suits are irrelevant) on top of the pack in the order 7, 5, 2, 8, 6, 3, A, 10, 9, 4 (so that the 7 is on top of the pack), and then replace the pack in its box.

Performance
Take the pack from its box and deal out the top ten cards, face down, on the table. Put the rest of the pack to one side and pick up the dealt cards (with the 7 now on the bottom). Hold the cards, face down, and then spell 'Ace', moving one card for each letter, from the top to the bottom of the packet. Turn the next card face up on the table, to show an Ace. Then spell 'two' and deal the next card, face up, to show a two. Continue to spell out the numbers up to nine and, in each case, the card of the matching value is dealt, face up, at the end of each spelling.

When there is just one card left (the ten), you can simply turn it face up on top of the pile of cards on the table. Alternatively, you can raise a smile from your audience by pretending to move one card from the top to the bottom of the packet, even though you have only one card in your hand!

Acrobats

A pack of cards is mixed by the performer, so that some cards are face up and some are face down. When the cards are spread out, they have all righted themselves.

Type	Skill demonstration
Skill level	Easy
Special techniques	None
Equipment	Pack of cards

Performance

Hold the pack in your left hand and push a few cards over into your right hand. Turn these cards over and put them back on top of the pack. Square up the pack and then push all the face-up cards, together with a few more of the following (face-down) cards, into your right hand. Turn the whole packet over and put it back on top of the pack. Continue this procedure until you have gone all the way through the pack. Now bring your right hand over the cards and separate them a little until you can see the first face-down card. Cut the pack at this point and turn the cards in your right hand over (try to do this while shielding the pack with your right hand if you can). It seems that the cards are well mixed, some face up and some face down. However, when you spread out the cards between your hands, the audience see that they have sorted themselves out, for they are all now face down.

Tips

Do this trick as a quick interlude between other tricks and perform it fairly quickly for the best effect.

Ad Lib

A spectator is asked to concentrate on any card, and its position, in a packet of cards. The packet of cards is then cut and shuffled by the spectator. Although he has no idea which card is in the spectator's mind, the performer's amazing mental powers are employed to name the card.

Type	Mind-reading
Skill level	Easy
Special techniques	None
Equipment	Pack of cards

Performance

Ask a spectator to shuffle the pack and then to hand the cards back to you. Take ten cards from the top of the pack and put the rest of the pack down on the table. (Do not count out the cards but rather take them in groups, so that it is not obvious how many cards you have taken.)

Spread the ten cards between your hands from left to right, so that the spectator can see all of them and, more importantly, you can see all the backs (see illustration 1 below).

①

Ask the spectator to think of any card and then note its position from the top card (the first card to his left). Turn your head away and request that he actually touches the card so at least one other spectator can see which card is in his mind.

For example, if the cards were as shown in illustration 2 overleaf and the spectator chose 9♠, he would have to remember that it was the seventh card from the top (the card furthest to the left from his viewpoint).

②

Turn your head back to face the audience and close the fan of cards. As you do so, put the tip of your right little finger between the fifth and sixth cards from the top (as the cards are well spread out, this is quite easy to do). Then cut the top five cards from the top to the bottom of the packet, as you say 'I'll just give the cards a cut to mix them up a bit.' Hand the packet of cards back to the spectator and ask him to transfer as many cards from the top to the bottom of the packet as the original position of his chosen card from the top card in the fan. So, in the example given above, he will take seven cards from the top to the bottom of the pack. Next take the packet of cards back from him, turn the cards face up and spread them out between the first finger and thumb of your right hand (see illustration 3 below).

③

Then, as you hand the cards back to the spectator, say 'There is no way that I could know which of these cards you have in mind but, just to make sure, will you please shuffle them.' While the cards were spread out in your hand, you will have had just enough time to look at, and remember, the fifth card from the top of the packet (the card furthest to your left in the fan), which is the spectator's card. You can now pretend to read the spectator's mind and announce, with great drama, the name of the card that he chose.

Tips
This is a good trick to perform when someone asks you to do a trick 'off the cuff', hence its title.

All in the Mind

The pack is shuffled by a spectator, and the card at the bottom of the pack is memorized. The pack is then put in its box, so that it cannot be seen by the performer. The spectator's mind is read, and the memorized card is named by the performer.

Type	Mind-reading
Skill level	Easy
Special techniques	None
Equipment	Pack of cards, card box, scissors

Preparation
Use a pair of scissors to cut a hole in the bottom right-hand corner of the back of the card box, and then put the cards back into the box.

Performance
Take the pack from the box, being careful not to reveal the hole in the box, and hand the cards to a spectator. Ask the spectator to shuffle the cards and then to look at, and memorize, the bottom card. Pick up the card box with the side containing the hole facing downwards, so that no one can see the hole, and ask the spectator to push the pack, face down, into the box. Close the box and put it on the table or in your pocket, first taking a quick look at the card index, which is visible through the hole (see illustration below).

This takes just a second and you now know the identity of the card in the spectator's mind. Pretend to concentrate very hard as you apparently read the spectator's mind and then, with as much drama as you can muster, reveal the name of the card.

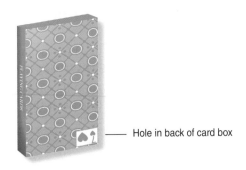

Hole in back of card box

Tips
Do not do this trick if there is anyone standing behind you, and do not let anyone handle the box or else the secret will be out!

Allakazam

Five cards glued together are shown to the audience. The group of cards is turned over and a spectator is invited to place a paper clip over the middle card. When the cards are turned face up again it is seen that the spectator has placed the clip nowhere near the centre card.

Type	Transposition
Skill level	Easy
Special techniques	None
Equipment	Five cards from an old pack, glue, paper clip

Preparation

Using an old pack of cards glue five cards together, each card overlapping the one to the left (see illustration below). Use a prominent card, such as a court card or an Ace for the card in the middle.

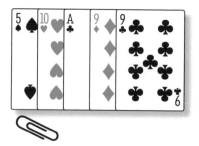

Performance

Show the group of glued cards to the audience and point out the prominent centre card.

Hand a spectator a paper clip and ask him to clip it onto the central card. But to make things a little more difficult you turn the group of cards face down.

The spectator places the clip on the middle card. Say the magic word 'Allakazam' and turn the cards face up again. It is seen that the clip is actually on the card second from the right of the spread.

Tips

If the cards are grouped closer together the clip will end up on the end card of the group.

It is a good idea to use a large, coloured paper clip, to make the effect more appealing to the eye.

Amazing Duet

> Two cards, chosen by two different spectators, are found in the pack by
> the performer even though the cards have been shuffled.

Type	Location
Skill level	Easy
Special techniques	Overhand shuffle
Equipment	Pack of cards

Preparation

Separate the red cards from the black cards, so that you have one pile of red
cards and one pile of black cards. Place the two halves of the pack together, but
do not mix the cards in any way, and then replace the pack in its box.

Performance

Take the pack from its box and, with the faces towards you, divide the pack into
two halves (one containing the red cards, the other the blacks), and then place
the two halves, face down and side by side, on the table. Invite a spectator to
take a card from one of the halves, and another spectator to take a card from the
other half. Ask them each to remember their card and then to push it into the
other half of the pack. Then ask each spectator to take one of the halves, give it
an overhand shuffle (see pxi) and place it back on the table. Pick up one half and
place it on top of the other, so that the pack is complete once again. Now all you
have to do is spread the cards, with the faces towards you, and pick out the only
black card in the red half and the only red card in the black half – they are the
chosen cards. While everyone is puzzling out how you did it, give the whole pack
a good shuffle, apparently in preparation for your next trick (but really to destroy
any evidence as to how the trick was done).

Astonishing Discovery

After a card has been chosen by a spectator and returned to the pack, the performer takes the cards behind his back. Batches of cards are then brought forward by the performer and, when the batch containing the spectator's card is indicated by him, the performer immediately identifies the chosen card in this batch.

Type	Location
Skill level	Moderate
Special techniques	None
Equipment	Pack of cards

Performance

Ask a spectator to shuffle the pack and then spread the cards face down. Then ask another spectator to choose a card, show it to the audience, and replace it anywhere in the pack.

As the card is returned to the pack, make a mental note of its position. Take the cards, put them behind your back and cut the pack just above the position that you noted. The spectator's card should now be at or near the top of the pack. Next, take a small number of cards (the exact number is not important) from the bottom of the pack and also one card from the top of the pack. Push the card from the top of the pack into the third position from the top in the batch of cards that you have just taken from the bottom of the pack.

Bring this batch of cards from behind your back and spread the cards, face up, on the table. Ask the spectator if he can see his chosen card and, if so, to concentrate hard on it. If the spectator says that he can see his card, you know that it must be the third card of the spread and you can pretend to read the spectator's mind to name it.

If the chosen card is not in this batch, do exactly the same with another batch of cards – taking some from the bottom of the pack and one from the top, and again inserting this top card into the third position from the top in the batch taken from the bottom of the pack. Continue doing this until the spectator says that he can see his card. As you know that it must be the third card of the spread you can then reveal its identity in the most mysterious manner you can muster.

Card in Thought

Nine cards are dealt out, face up, on the table by a spectator. One of the cards is then chosen by another spectator while the performer's back is turned. The performer's mental powers are then employed to identify the chosen card.

Type	Mind-reading
Skill level	Easy
Special techniques	None
Equipment	Pack of cards, a confederate

Preparation
In agreement with your confederate, mentally divide a playing card into nine parts (see illustration below).

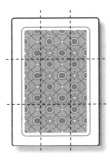

Performance
Ask your confederate (the audience, of course, do not realize that you are working together) to shuffle the cards and then to deal nine cards, face up, on the table in three rows of three cards each. Then ask a second spectator to point to any card while your back is turned to the audience. When you turn back round, your confederate, who is still holding the pack, puts his thumb on the back of the top card, its position on the card representing the place occupied by the chosen card on the table.

A quick glance at the position of his thumb is all you will need to identify which card was selected. However, take your time as you pretend to concentrate hard and then slowly, and mysteriously, name the chosen card.

Catch Them

Two cards are shown to the audience and are then pushed into the pack in different positions. The cards are taken by the performer and thrown onto the table. However, two of these remain in his hand – the very two cards that were shown earlier.

Type	Skill demonstration
Skill level	Moderate
Special techniques	None
Equipment	Pack of cards

Preparation
Put 8♣ on the top of the pack and 7♠ on the bottom of the pack, and then replace the pack in its box.

Performance
Take the pack from its box and then look through the cards and remove 8♠ and 7♣. Show these two cards to the audience – but only briefly, and do not name them. Then push these cards, face down, in different positions in the pack.

Hold the pack firmly between your forefinger and thumb and give it a sharp downward flick, so that all the cards fall on the table with the exception of the top and bottom cards which remain between your fingers. Turn the two cards face up and show them to the audience, as if they were the same two cards you put in the pack earlier. Then, gather up all the cards and go on to another trick.

Tips
With practice, you can place 8♣ and 7♠ on the top and bottom of the pack while doing another trick, so you do not have to prepare the pack in advance. Remember not to name the cards you are using: just show them briefly to the audience before pushing them into the pack.

Changing Places

A card is chosen by a spectator, shown to the audience, and is then replaced by him in the pack. A card is taken in turn by the performer, shown to the audience, and put in the performer's pocket. The spectator is then asked to look through the pack for his card, but it cannot be found. Instead the performer's card is found, reversed, in the pack, and the spectator's card is discovered in the performer's pocket.

Type	Transposition
Skill level	Moderate
Special techniques	Double lift, secret reversal
Equipment	Pack of cards

Performance

Ask a spectator to take a card and to show it to the rest of the audience before handing it, face down, to you. Then say that you are going to push the card into the pack but, to make sure that it goes into a random position, you are going to do this with the cards held behind your back.

Hold the pack behind your back and simply put the chosen card on top of the pack before bringing your hands in front of you once again. Next, choose a card by turning the top card of the pack over, and show it to the audience. However, what you have actually done is a double lift (see pxx), to show the second card to the audience. Turn the card (in fact, two cards) face down again on top of the pack, and then put the top card (the spectator's card) in your pocket without letting the audience see its face.

Then apparently cut the pack and hand it to the spectator, asking him to look through the cards to find his chosen card. In fact, while you were cutting the pack, you performed the secret reversal (see pxxv) so that your card is now reversed in the pack.

The spectator looks through the pack and cannot find his card but he does find your card reversed in the pack. You then ask him to take the card from your pocket, and it turns out to be his card: the two cards have changed places!

Tips

You could, if you wish, ask the spectator to write his initials on his card and, in turn, you could write your initials on your own card. This does make the trick more dramatic, but of course has the disadvantage of destroying two cards each time you perform the trick.

Coincidence

Two cards are placed, face up, on the table by the performer and the pack is then handed to a spectator, who deals cards until he decides to stop. The pack is then reassembled and further cards are dealt until the spectator decides to stop dealing for a second time. When the cards are examined, it is found that the spectator has stopped at the 'twins' of the cards the performer predicted.

Type	Mind-reading
Skill level	Easy
Special techniques	None
Equipment	Pack of cards

Performance

Ask a spectator to shuffle the pack and then to return the cards to you. Spread the cards with their faces towards you and say that you are going to forecast something that will happen in the future. What you really do is look at the top and bottom cards of the pack and place their 'twins', face up, on the table. So if, for example, the top and bottom cards are J♣ and 5♦, you take out J♠ and 5♥ and place them on the table. Hand the pack back to the spectator and ask him to deal cards, face down, on the table and to stop dealing whenever he wants. When he stops, place the twin of the original bottom card (in the above example this will be 5♥), face up, on top of the dealt cards and ask him to place the cards he still holds on top of the face-up card. Then ask him to pick up the whole pack, deal a few more cards, face down, on the table and, once again, stop whenever he wants. When he does so, you put the other face-up card (J♠ in the above example) on top of the dealt cards and ask him to place the balance of the cards he holds on top of that.

Next, ask the spectator to pick up the whole pack and to spread the cards out, face down, from left to right on the table. There will be two face-up cards in the pack (the two you put on the table at the start of the trick). Ask the spectator to pick out the card to the right of one of the face-up cards and then to turn it over – it is the twin of that face-up card. Tell him to turn over the card to the right of the other face-up card and, again, it is the twin of that card. (So, in the above example, J♠ and 5♥ will be face up and next to them will be J♣ and 5♦.)

Tips

Emphasize the fact that the cards are in the spectator's hands throughout and that it is he who decides where to stop on each deal.

18

Colour Confusion

The cards are mixed, so that some are face up and some are face down. Amazingly, they are all then separated out into their respective colours, with the exception of two previously-chosen cards.

Type	Transformation
Skill level	Advanced
Special techniques	Weave shuffle
Equipment	Pack of cards

Preparation
Separate the red cards from the black cards, place the red cards on top of the black and then put the whole pack into its box.

Performance
Take the cards from their box and cut the pack into two exact halves, so that the red cards are in one half and the black cards are in the other half. Place the half containing the black cards down on the table and spread the red cards across the table, face down. Ask a spectator to pull out six or seven of these cards, face down, and then gather up the remainder of the spread cards and put them back down in a pile on the table. Now ask the spectator to take any card from the few he has removed, turn it face up, remember it and then place it, face up, anywhere in the removed group. You now turn to a second spectator and do exactly the same with the half of the pack containing the black cards – you spread the black cards, face down, on the table, the spectator removes several cards, chooses one of these, turns it over and replaces it, face up, in the group of removed cards. In the meantime, you again gather up the spread cards and place them in a pile to one side. Now take the cards from the first spectator, turn them over, face up, and weave shuffle (see pxii) them into the face-down black half of the pack (don't forget that the audience has no knowledge of the fact that the cards have been pre-arranged). Take the group of cards from the second spectator, turn them face up and weave them into the face-down red half of the pack. Tell the audience that the cards are now well mixed 'but to make quite sure, I will mix them up well and truly'. Then pick up the red half, turn it face up and weave shuffle it (see pxii) and the black face-down half together.

Now spread the cards out between your hands and show that all the red cards are now, much to the surprise of the audience, face up, with the exception of one black card – the card chosen by the second spectator. Turn the pack over, spread them out, and all the face-up cards are black, except the red card chosen by the first spectator!

Countdown Prediction

The pack is shuffled by the performer and then a prediction is written and given to a spectator to hold. Ten cards are dealt by a second spectator and these are then shuffled. Four of the ten cards are then placed, face up, on the table. The appropriate number of cards are dealt, face down, on top of the cards, so that the value of each face-up card and the number of cards dealt on top of it makes ten. The values of the face-up cards are totalled, the spectator counts down the pack to that number, and the card at that number is shown. The prediction is then opened by the first spectator, to reveal the name of the very card being shown.

Type	Mind-reading
Skill level	Moderate
Special techniques	Glimpse
Equipment	Pack of cards, pencil, piece of paper

Preparation
Take two cards from the pack, put them in your pocket and put the pack back in its box.

Performance
Take the pack from its box, give the cards a good shuffle and glimpse (see pxxiii) the bottom card. Then place the pack on the table, pick up the paper and pencil and write down the name of the glimpsed card on the piece of paper. Be very careful not to let anyone see what you have written. Fold the paper and hand it to a spectator for safekeeping. Ask a second spectator to deal ten cards from the top of the pack, face down, onto the table, and then to put the rest of the pack to one side. Next ask the spectator to shuffle his ten cards and to put any four of them, face up, on the table. Take the remaining six cards from him, pick up the rest of the pack, put it on top of the six cards, and then hand the pack to the spectator. Ask him to deal cards, face down, on top of the four face-up cards, to make piles totalling ten, using the value of the face-up card as the starting point. If, for example, the face-up card is a three, he will put seven cards on top of it, to make the total of ten. If the face-up card is a picture card, he will put no cards on it as the picture cards count as ten for this trick.

Next ask the spectator to add together the values of the four face-up cards (see illustration opposite, where the value is 23) and then to count down to that number in the remainder of the pack, which he is still holding.

Then ask him to show the audience the card at that number. Turn to the first spectator and ask him to read out the name of the card written on the prediction. This proves that you can foresee the future, because the cards are one and the same!

Tips

As you will still have two cards in your pocket at the end of the trick, you could follow it with the next trick, 'Countdown Prediction Repeat'. As a general rule, it is bad practice to repeat a trick but 'Countdown Prediction Repeat' is sufficiently different from this trick for you to make an exception in this case.

Countdown Prediction Repeat

After the pack has been shuffled, a prediction is written on a piece of paper by the performer. The paper is then folded and handed to a spectator for safekeeping. The pack is shuffled by a second spectator and 20 cards are dealt off and shuffled. Three of the 20 cards are then placed, face up, on the table and the pack is reassembled. The appropriate number of cards is then dealt, face down, by the second spectator, on top of the three face-up cards, so that the sum of the value of each face-up card and the number of cards dealt on top of it is ten. The values of the face-up cards are then added together. The spectator counts down the pack to that number, and the card at that number is shown. The prediction is then opened by the second spectator and the name of the card written on it is seen to be the very card just arrived at.

Type	Mind-reading
Skill level	Moderate
Special techniques	Glimpse
Equipment	Pack of cards, pencil, piece of paper

Preparation

Take two cards from the pack, place them in your pocket and then replace the rest of the pack in its box.

Performance

Take the pack from its box, give the cards a good shuffle and then place them on the table, glimpsing (see pxxiii) the bottom card as you do so. Then pick up the pencil and paper, write down the name of the glimpsed card (being careful not to let anyone see what you have written), fold the paper and give it to a spectator to look after.

Ask a second spectator to deal 20 cards from the top of the pack, to shuffle them, and then to put any three, face up, on the table. Then pick up the pack and put it on top of the cards that the spectator is still holding, as you ask him to deal cards, face down, on each of the face-up cards, to make the total up to ten, taking the value of the face-up card as the starting point. So, if the face-up card is a six, for example, the spectator deals four cards on top of it. Picture cards count as ten, so no cards are dealt on them. Now add together the values of the face-up cards and ask the spectator to count out and deal cards, face down, from the top of the pack to that number. Ask the first spectator to read out the name of the card you wrote on the piece of paper, and then ask the second spectator to show the card at the number he has arrived at – it is the very card that you predicted!

Detector

The pack is divided into two, one half being taken by a spectator, and the other half by the performer. A card is chosen by the spectator from his half of the pack, and this is then returned to the half-pack. A card is taken in turn, by the performer, from his half of the pack, and this is then pushed into the spectator's half-pack. The audience are told that the performer's card will end up next to the card chosen by the spectator. This proves not to be the case, but – even more impressively – the card inserted by the performer magically turns into the card chosen by the spectator.

Type	Transposition
Skill level	Moderate
Special techniques	Break control, palm
Equipment	Pack of cards

Performance

Ask a spectator to shuffle the cards and to give you roughly half of the pack, which you then place in your pocket. You then take the spectator's half of the pack and ask him to choose any card, look at it, remember it and show it to the audience, without letting you see it. Ask him to return the card to his half-pack and secretly bring it to the top using the break control (see pxxii).

Tell the audience that you are going to use one of the cards from your half of the pack to find the spectator's card. As you are saying this, palm off the top card (see pxxii) of the spectator's half-pack into your right hand and ask the spectator to shuffle the cards and then hold them face up. Place your right hand in your pocket and, when the spectator has finished shuffling, bring out the (face-down) palmed card (which you pretend that you have taken from the half-pack in your pocket), and push it into the centre of the spectator's (face-up) half-pack. Tell the audience that this card will be placed next to the card chosen by the spectator.

Spread the spectator's half-pack face up until the face-down card (the card you inserted) comes into view. Say 'Here is my card, so the card next to it is your chosen card.' The spectator will say 'No, it's not' so you spread out a few more face-up cards and ask 'Well, is my card anywhere near your card?' and again the spectator will say 'No'. Pull out the face-down card and say something like 'That is strange, it usually works. What was your card?' When the spectator names his card, turn over the card in your hand and the audience will see that it is the spectator's chosen card!

Dissolved

A card is chosen by a spectator and is then placed beneath a handkerchief. The handkerchief, with the card inside, is handed to another spectator who holds it while water is poured by the performer from a jug into a tumbler. The handkerchief is then taken by the performer and is held above the tumbler while the card is gradually pushed into the water. When the handkerchief is lifted, the card is nowhere to be seen but it is later found in the performer's pocket.

Type	Transposition
Skill level	Advanced
Special techniques	Palm
Equipment	Pack of cards, piece of clear celluloid, tumbler, jug of water, handkerchief

Preparation
Cut the piece of celluloid to the size and shape of a playing card and then put this in your right coat pocket. Put the handkerchief in the same pocket and place the tumbler and the jug of water on the table.

Performance
Ask a spectator to take any card from the pack and to hand it to you. While he is doing this, put your right hand into your right pocket and bring out the handkerchief, at the same time palming (see pxxii) the piece of celluloid in your right hand. Then give the spectator the handkerchief to examine, as you take the card from him with your left hand, immediately transferring it, face down, into your right palm, and placing it over the celluloid. Show the card to the audience – the celluloid, being transparent, will not be noticed – and then take the handkerchief from the spectator and throw it over the card (and the celluloid, of course). Next, hand the handkerchief and card to a second spectator to hold. In fact, what you really do is palm the card in your left hand so that it is the piece of celluloid that the second spectator can feel through the handkerchief.

Turn your body to the left as you pick up the jug and fill the tumbler with water and, at the same time, secretly drop the palmed card into your left jacket pocket. Next, take the handkerchief containing the piece of celluloid from the spectator, and drape it over the tumbler. Move your hand down slowly, apparently pushing the card into the water. Wait for a few seconds, and then, with a dramatic gesture, whip away the handkerchief. The card has apparently vanished, for the celluloid is not visible in the water. Finally, ask the first spectator to reach into your left jacket pocket and take out his card, which has travelled there by magic.

Tips
Make sure the tumbler is big enough to immerse the celluloid in water.

Ditto

Four cards are chosen freely from the pack, each by a different spectator. When the cards are turned face up, they are seen, by a magical coincidence, to be the four Aces.

Type	Coincidence
Skill level	Advanced
Special techniques	False shuffle
Equipment	Pack of cards

Preparation
Place the four Aces on top of the pack and then put the pack back in its box.

Performance
Take the pack from its box and give the cards a false shuffle (see pxii), so that the four Aces remain on the top of the pack. Fan the cards out face down and ask four spectators each to pull just one card halfway from the fan.

Next, close up the fan of cards, but leave the four chosen cards sticking out. Hold the pack in your left hand, with your thumb on one side and three fingers on the opposite side and your left forefinger curled underneath the pack. Then bring your right hand over, so that it is holding the protruding cards between your thumb and little finger, with your other three fingers at the front, concealing the cards and the following moves from view.

With your right hand, pull the protruding cards away from you and out of the pack. This movement provides perfect cover for your left thumb to allow most of the pack to drop down (see illustration below), and the cards from your right hand are pushed into the gap thus formed.

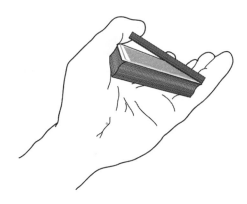

Immediately, allow the top part of the pack (containing the four Aces) to drop down onto the cards selected by the spectators, and then deal the top four cards, face down, on the table.

You will need to practise this whole sequence of moves so that your audience believe that you have simply taken the chosen cards in your right hand and placed them on top of the pack before dealing them onto the table.

Make sure that you emphasize the fact that the four spectators had a perfectly free choice of cards, and then dramatically turn over the four cards on the table to show that they are the four Aces.

Tips

The transfer of the four chosen cards – inserting them into the pack and then dealing the top four cards – must be done in one continuous and smooth movement. It requires some practice to get the timing and rhythm right, and you must also learn to look at the audience and not at your hands as you do it.

Double Deal

Five rows of five cards are dealt by the performer and a spectator is asked to concentrate on any card and to indicate which row it is in. Once again, the cards are picked up and dealt out, and the spectator is asked which row contains his card. The spectator's card is then identified by the performer.

Type	Location
Skill level	Easy
Special techniques	None
Equipment	Pack of cards

Performance

From a shuffled pack deal out, face up, 25 cards in five rows of five cards. Now ask a spectator to concentrate on any one of the cards, and to tell you which row it is in. You must remember the card at the left-hand end of the chosen row.

If, for example, the cards were laid out as shown in illustration 1 opposite, and he says that his card is in the second row, the card you remember will be 3 ♦.

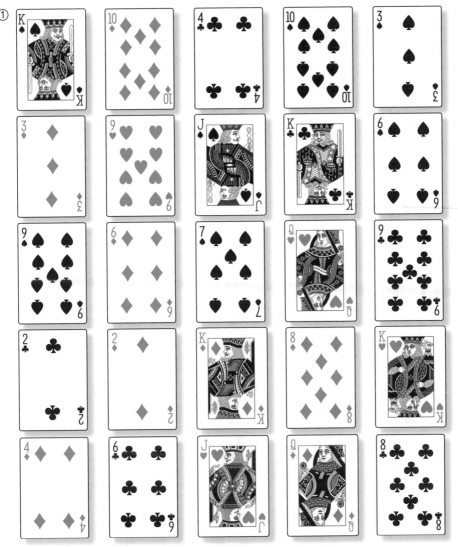

You then pick up all the cards, face up, starting at the bottom right-hand corner and working up the column, placing each card you lift beneath the ones you are already holding. When you reach the top of the column, go to the bottom of the next column to the left and continue in this fashion until all the cards have been picked up.

Then turn the packet of cards face down and deal out all the cards, again in five rows of five cards, turning them face up as you do so. Once more, ask the spectator to indicate which row contains his card. The chosen card will be in the column headed by the card you remembered earlier. So, as soon as you know the row, you can identify the chosen card, and you can then pretend to read the spectator's mind to reveal it.

Using the layout of cards shown in illustration 1 above, after you have dealt out **27** the cards again, the layout will be as in illustration 2 below. Therefore, if the spectator says, for example, that his card is in row three, you will know that he is thinking of J♠.

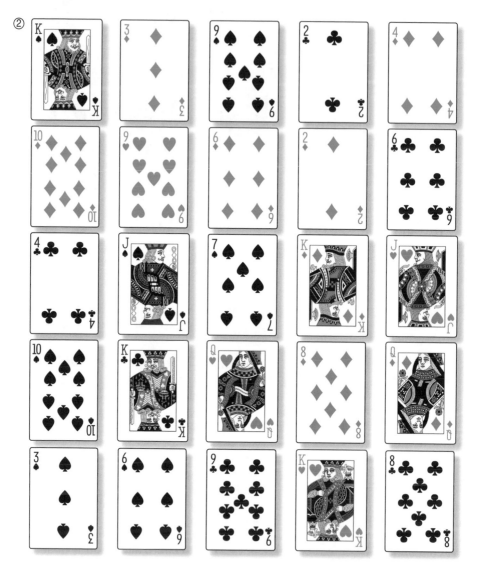

Double Turnover

Half of the pack is taken by a spectator, and the other half by the performer. A card is then taken, and memorized, by each of them from their respective half of the pack, and is returned to the other person's half-pack. The spectator's packet is divided into two, with one half, face up, on top of the performer's face-down cards and the other half, face up, beneath them, so that the performer's cards are sandwiched between those of the spectator. The chosen cards are then named and the pack of cards is correctly reordered, except for the two chosen cards which are now reversed.

Type	Transposition / location
Skill level	Moderate
Special techniques	None
Equipment	Pack of cards

Preparation
Turn over the bottom card of the pack and make a mental note of it, before replacing it, face up, on the bottom. Let us assume that this card is 2♥.

Performance
Place the pack on the table and ask a spectator to take off about half of the cards, and to spread them out, face down. Then ask him to take out any card and to put it on the table, before squaring up the rest of the cards. You do the same with the other half of the pack, being careful not to expose the reversed card at the bottom. Ask the spectator to take a look at the card he has put on the table and to remember it. You apparently do the same with your chosen card, but just pretend to memorize it. At the same time, turn over the cards you are holding, so that the reversed card is now face down on top of a face-up packet.

Next pick up your card from the table and give it to the spectator, telling him not to look at it but just to push it, face down, into his half of the pack. You do the same with his card, pushing it, face down, into your half of the pack, being careful to keep the cards neatly squared (so that the reversed cards are not visible to the spectator or audience). Now ask the spectator for half of his cards which you place, face up, on top of the cards you are holding. Then ask him for his remaining cards which you place, face up, beneath your cards.

Turn the pack over and ask the spectator for the name of his card, as you say that your card is 2♥ (the card you reversed before the trick started). Spread all the cards on the table and the audience will be amazed to see that the pack has magically righted itself except for the two chosen cards, which are face up in the face-down pack.

Dual Identity

With the cards held behind his back, the performer's magical skills are employed to identify a mystery card that is being held by a spectator.

Type	Location
Skill level	Moderate
Special techniques	Stacked pack
Equipment	Pack of cards

Preparation
Stack the whole pack in an Eight Kings sequence (see pxix).

Performance
Turn away from the audience, holding the pack behind your back. Ask a spectator to pull out any card from the pack, to show it to the audience and then to place it, face down, on the table, all before you turn back round to face the audience. With the cards still held behind your back, cut the pack at the point from which the card was taken. Then, count down four cards from this point and throw the fourth card onto the table face down. Count down a further nine cards and place this card, face down, on the table as well.

Ask the spectator for the name of his card and then turn over the two cards you have placed on the table – one of these will match the suit of the card that he chose, and the other will match its value.

Because of the way the pack is stacked, the fourth card after the spectator's card will be of the same suit as his card and the 13th card after his card will be of the same value as his card.

Faulty Follower

Five cards are dealt for a spectator, and then another five cards for the performer himself. Cards are moved by the performer from the top to the bottom of his packet, some face down and some face up, and the same is done by the spectator. When the performer's cards are spread out, they are all face down, while the spectator has one face-up card in his packet. Even when the sequence is repeated, with the spectator following each move carefully, the performer's cards are all face down but the spectator has, again, got one card face up!

Type	Skill demonstration
Skill level	Easy
Special techniques	None
Equipment	Pack of cards, double-backed card

Preparation
Make a double-backed card and place it in the ninth position from the top of the pack. A double-backed card is simply two old cards glued face to face to make a single card that has a back design on both sides. (This design must, of course, be the same as the ordinary cards you use.) Double-backed cards, with only the thickness of a single card, can be obtained from most magic shops.

Performance
Deal five cards from the top of the pack and hand them, face down, to a spectator. Then deal five cards for yourself (this puts the double-backed card in the second position in your packet of cards). Fan out your cards, face down (see illustration 1 below), and ask the spectator to do the same with his cards, so that the audience can see that all the cards are face down. Close up the fan.

①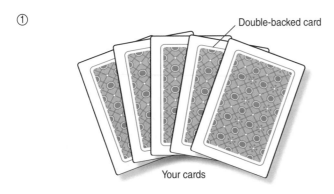

Double-backed card

Your cards

31

Now ask the spectator to copy what you do exactly, as you turn the top card of your packet face up and then put it to the bottom of the packet. Take the next card from the top of your packet and put it, face down, on the bottom of the packet. The spectator then does the same.

Now take the next top card, turn it face up and put it to the bottom, and follow this by taking the next card from the top to the bottom, without turning it over.

At this point, make sure that the spectator has followed your instructions so far by fanning out your five cards, to show three face-down and two face-up cards (see illustration 2 below), and then asking the spectator to do the same: the pattern of his cards does indeed match yours.

②   Double-backed card

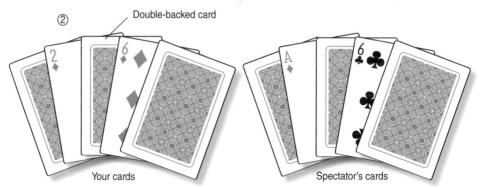

Your cards   Spectator's cards

Remind the spectator to follow your moves exactly and then close up your fan of cards. Turn the top card face up and replace it, face up, on top of your packet of cards.

Now turn the whole packet over in your hand, and turn the new top card face down and put it back on the packet.

Then spread out your cards, to show that they are all face down. However, when the spectator does the same, he has one card face up in his packet (see illustration 3 below).

③   Double-backed card

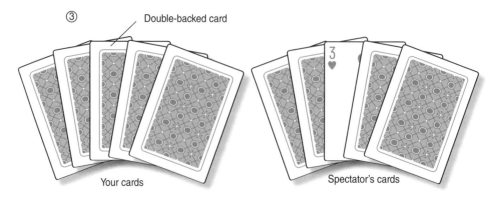

Your cards   Spectator's cards

Ask the spectator to turn that card face down and offer to try the whole thing again. For this second performance, there is an extra initial move for you to make: you must take the top card of your packet and put it, face down, on the bottom, as this will bring the double-backed card into the correct position. This enables the whole sequence of moves just described to be repeated. However, once again, your cards end up all face down, while the spectator still has one face-up card in his packet!

Find the Aces

The pack is shuffled four times and, after each shuffle, an Ace is discovered at the top of the pack.

Type	Skill demonstration
Skill level	Moderate
Special techniques	Overhand shuffle
Equipment	Pack of cards containing a short card

Preparation
Put the four Aces on top of the pack and the short card (see pxxiv) on top of them.

Performance
Give the cards an overhand shuffle (see pxi), making sure that the first batch of cards you drop contains at least the top five cards. Then cut the cards so as to bring the short card to the top of the pack. Pick off the top (short) card and use it as a lever to turn over the top card of the pack, which will be one of the Aces. Drop this Ace, face up, on the table. Replace the short card, face down, on top of the pack and repeat the whole sequence again three more times to produce the other three Aces.

Fingertip Fooler

Cards are taken from the pack at random by the performer, and his fingertips are used to 'read' the name of each card even though the backs are towards him.

Type	Mind-reading
Skill level	Moderate
Special techniques	None
Equipment	Pack of cards

Performance

Ask a spectator to shuffle the pack and then to hand you any card, face down. Take the card, its back towards you, in your right hand, with your thumb at the bottom short end and your fingers at the top short end. Hold the card so that the audience can see its face, and then bring your left forefinger up to touch the top index of the card (see illustrations 1 and 2 below).

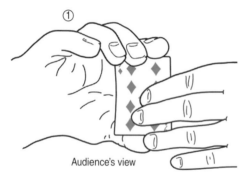

Audience's view

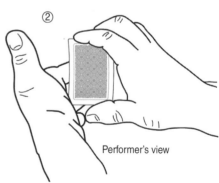

Performer's view

At this point, much of your left hand is actually covering the card. So, in the meantime, your right fingers can secretly exert pressure on both ends of the card, bending it backwards until you can see the bottom index (see illustration 3 opposite).

③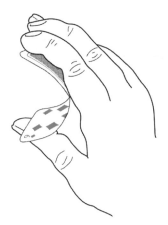

As soon as you see the index, allow the card to straighten and then announce, in the most mysterious manner you can muster, the name of the card. Then either return the card to the pack or drop it onto the table and repeat the trick with two or three more cards (but no more than this, or you may be caught out).

Tips
Try not to make it obvious that you are looking at the card at any stage – a quick glance is all you will need. The main secret here is not the method (ie the bending of the card which should be invisible to the audience), but your ability to convince the audience that you really have amazing powers.

Flip

A spectator is handed the four Aces and is asked by the performer to mix them up and to reverse one of them in the packet. The packet of four cards is placed in a card box and shaken. When the cards are taken out of the box, the reversed Ace has righted itself and the other Ace of the same colour is now reversed in the packet.

Type	Transposition
Skill level	Easy
Special techniques	None
Equipment	Pack of cards

Performance
Take the four Aces from the pack and put the rest of the pack to one side. Show a spectator the Aces, with the two reds together and the two blacks together

35

(see illustration 1), and say that you want him to mix them up behind his back.

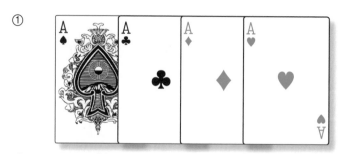

As if to demonstrate this, you turn the four cards face down and take them behind your back to mix them up. However, what you really do when the cards are behind your back is to turn the two bottom cards face up and then replace them under the other two face-down cards so that, unbeknown to the audience, the cards are now as in illustration 2.

Square up the packet behind your back and then hand the packet of cards to the spectator. After he has mixed the cards behind his back, tell him to turn over the whole packet three times, take out any card and bring it forward. If the card is face up, tell him to remember it, then to turn it face down and to push it anywhere in the packet (which he is still holding behind his back). If the card he selects is face down, tell him to turn it face up, remember it, and then to put it anywhere in the packet, still face up.

Ask him to mix the packet of cards some more, then hand him the card box behind his back and ask him to drop the cards into the box and close it. Take the card box from him and give it a shake, as you remind the audience that the card chosen by the spectator has been reversed in the packet (let us assume that it is A♣). Tell the audience that, even though the Aces are safely in the box, you still have power over them and that you can prove that power by righting the first Ace and reversing the other Ace of the same colour. Ask the spectator to remove the packet of cards from the box and to spread the cards out. There is still one card reversed in the packet, but it is now the partner of the one originally reversed (A♠).

Tips

No matter which card is reversed at the start of the trick, its partner will always be the one reversed at the end. However, you must make your instructions clear to ensure success.

Flushed

All of the high cards are taken from a shuffled pack by the performer. They are then held behind his back, and each suit is brought forward in turn as a royal flush.

Type	Skill demonstration
Skill level	Moderate
Special techniques	Riffle shuffle
Equipment	Pack of cards

Preparation

Go through the pack and remove all the tens, Jacks, Queens, Kings and Aces. Arrange the diamonds and spades so that the suits alternate (ie a diamond is followed by a spade, which is then followed by another diamond, and so on) then alternate the hearts and clubs in the same way. Don't worry about the values of the cards. In the end, your set-up will be similar to that shown in illustration 1 below. Put these 20 cards on top of the pack.

Performance

Cut the pack in the middle and give the cards a riffle shuffle (see pxi). Although this is a genuine shuffle, it separates, but does not disturb, the sequence of the 20 cards. Then spread out the cards with the faces towards you. Starting at the right-hand end, push the cards to the right and take out every high card (ie ten, Jack, Queen, King and Ace) as you come to it and place it face down on the table. Tell the audience that you are taking out all the high cards. The amazing part of this procedure is that the cards on the table are now in the original stacked order.

Put the main part of the pack to one side and pick up the packet of cards from the table. Tell the audience that you will 'mix them up a little' as you deal out the cards in two piles. Then, place the right pile on top of the left pile. Next, hold the packet of cards behind your back and take the first five cards between your right forefinger and second finger, the second group of five between your forefinger and thumb, the third group between your second and third fingers, and the final group between your third and fourth fingers (see illustration 2 below).

②

The first group are all spades, the second clubs, the third hearts and the fourth diamonds. Ask a spectator to call out any suit, and you can instantly bring forward a royal flush of that suit. Do the same with the other suits and you have accomplished yet another miracle!

Follow the Leader

Ten cards – A♥ to 5♥ and A♠ to 5♠ – are shown to the audience by the performer. The two Aces are then placed, face up, on the table as red and black 'leader' cards. In spite of the fact that the red cards and the black cards are moved around, as are the leader cards, the cards always follow their leader.

Type	Transposition
Skill level	Moderate
Special techniques	Glide
Equipment	Pack of cards

Performance

Go through the pack and take out ten cards: A♥ to 5♥ and A♠ to 5♠. Place the two Aces, face up, on the table and arrange the remaining eight cards in this order: 5♥, 4♥, 3♥, 2♥, 3♠, 4♠, 5♠, 2♠. Display these cards in a fan formation to the audience (see illustration 1 opposite), pointing out that there are four red cards and four black cards, but without drawing their attention to the sequence of the cards.

Close the fan of cards and hold them, face down, in your left hand, as you say to the audience 'The black cards go with the black Ace.' As you are talking, draw four cards, one at a time, from the bottom of the packet and place them alongside A♠. However, what you are really doing is performing the glide (see pxx), holding back the bottom card all the time, so that you are actually placing three black cards and one red card on the table.

Square up the cards in your left hand, bringing the bottom card forward and back into line with the others. Then deal the rest of the cards from the top of the packet onto the table, next to A♥, as you say 'And all the red cards go with their red leader.' The audience believe that there are now four black cards alongside the black Ace, and four red cards next to the red Ace (see illustration 2). In fact, each pile has only three cards of the correct colour and one card of the other colour.

Now switch the positions of the two leader cards, as you say 'No matter how the Aces are changed, the other cards will always follow their leader.' Then turn over the top card of each of the face-down piles, to show that the twos have, indeed, followed their leader. Place each of these cards, according to their colour, on top of the corresponding leader cards. Then switch the positions of the two face-down piles and turn over the top card of each: each will be a three and will match the colour of the leader card. Again, place each card on the corresponding face-up pile.

To confuse things even further, you next exchange the position of a face-down pile and a face-up pile that are diagonally opposite one another (see illustration 3).

③

When you turn over the top card of each face-down pile to show the two fours, the colour of each card again matches that of the leader. Once again, place these top cards on the face-up pile. Finally, change the positions of the other face-up pile and the face-down card which is diagonally opposite (see illustration 4).

④
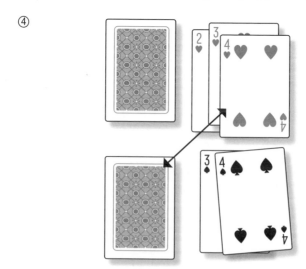

To the audience's amazement, when the two remaining single cards (fives) are turned over, they too have followed their leader! (See illustration opposite.)

Four Burglars

To illustrate the performer's story about four burglars, the Jacks are pushed into different parts of the pack and then, magically, jump together to the top of the pack.

Type	Transposition
Skill level	Moderate
Special techniques	None
Equipment	Pack of cards

Performance

Remove the four Jacks from the pack, but secretly take three more cards as well. Fan out the Jacks, with the other three cards hidden behind one of them (see illustration below), and show the cards to the audience.

Three cards hidden behind this card

Then close up the fan and place these seven cards (the audience, of course, believe there are only four cards), face down, on top of the pack.

Take the first card from the top of the pack and push it, face down, into the pack about ten cards from the bottom, leaving it sticking out a little. Do the same with the next card taken from the top, placing it about 20 cards from the bottom, again leaving it protruding slightly from the pack. Take the next card from the top of the pack and push it into the pack about 30 cards from the bottom and leave it sticking out like the other two cards. Turn the top card over, to show that it is a Jack (the audience believe that the cards sticking out from the pack are also Jacks) and then turn it back, face down, on the top of the pack.

Next push all the protruding cards into the pack, so it seems that the four Jacks are now distributed evenly throughout the pack. Finally, turn over the top four cards, one by one, and the four Jacks have, apparently, made their way back to the top of the pack.

Tips

This trick is best done accompanied by a story about four burglars (the Jacks) who decide to burgle a house (the pack). They all get onto the roof of the house, then one goes down to the basement, a second goes into the living room and the third breaks a window to get into a bedroom. As you say this, you illustrate where each of them is in the house by pushing the cards into the pack in the various positions described above. The fourth burglar stays on the roof to act as a lookout and, as you tell the audience this, you turn over the top card to show that it is a Jack. At this point, push all the cards flush so that it appears that the Jacks are spread through the pack. Suddenly, a police car arrives on the scene, so the burglar on the roof calls out to his accomplices, who run up to the roof and then slide down a drainpipe to make their escape (as you say this, you deal the four Jacks from the top of the pack and onto the table).

Four Tops

A shuffled pack is cut into four piles by a spectator and then the performer's psychic abilities are used to name the top card of each pile.

Type	Mind-reading
Skill level	Moderate
Special techniques	Glimpse, false shuffle
Equipment	Pack of cards

Performance

Hand the pack of cards to a spectator and ask him to shuffle it thoroughly.

Take the pack and tell the audience that you are going to try an experiment in telepathy (mind-reading). While you are talking, casually tilt the pack so that you can get a quick glimpse (see pxxiii) of the bottom card. Continue talking as you give the cards an overhand shuffle, making sure that the last throw of the shuffle consists of just one card (see pxi). This means that you have secretly brought the card you glimpsed to the top of the pack.

Ask a second spectator to place the pack on the table and then divide it into four piles. In the meantime, keep a track of the original top card (let's assume that it is 4♥).

Place your fingertips on top of any of the other piles and say 'four of Hearts' (or whatever card you glimpsed). Pick up the card and look at it, but do not say anything – just give a quiet smile. Let us assume that this card is Q♠. Keep it in your hand but do not let anyone see it.

Touch the top card of another pile and say 'Queen of Spades'. Pick up this card (let's say it's 9♦) and place it on top of the one you have in your hand. Then, touch another pile and say 'nine of Diamonds' and again take the top card (let's say it's 5♣) and put it on top of the cards in your hand.

Now touch the last pile (the original top of the pack with the card, 4♥, you glimpsed at the beginning) and say 'five of Clubs'. Take off the top card and place it beneath the cards you have in your hand.

Pause for a second or two and then spread the four cards from your hand face up on the table to show that they really are the four cards you have named!

Tips

As a variation of this trick, do not divide the pack into four but simply have four spectators each take a card from a fan of cards and place it, unseen, on the table. You then reveal the identity of the four cards, starting with the last one chosen. The first card is actually forced (see pxiii) so you know what it is but, as in the trick just described, it is the last one to be picked up.

Hand of Aces

The four Aces are shown and are put into the pack, which is then shuffled. Four hands of four cards are then dealt out by the performer. Three of the hands are made up of indifferent cards, but the performer's hand consists of the four Aces.

Type	Skill demonstration
Skill level	Advanced
Special techniques	Thumb count, false shuffle
Equipment	Pack of cards

Performance

Remove the four Aces from the pack and show them to the audience. Then, hand them to a spectator, asking him to pick any one of them. As this is happening, secretly thumb count three cards from the top of the pack. To perform a thumb count hold the pack in your left hand with the ball of your left thumb pushing down at the top-left corner. Your left forefinger should be beneath the pack pushing upwards. Cards are released singly by the thumb until the desired number has been counted. You then push your thumb further into the pack to create a gap (magicians call this a 'break') between the cards just counted and the rest of the pack (see illustration below).

Then, take the chosen Ace from the spectator and push it into the break beneath the top three cards, leaving it sticking out of the pack for the audience to see. Ask the spectator for another Ace and take it in your right hand as your left thumb counts down three more cards and keeps a small break. The first, protruding, Ace helps to conceal the thumb count and the subsequent break. Next, push the second Ace into the break, again leaving part of the card sticking out.

Do exactly the same with the last two Aces, leaving three cards between the second and third and also between the third and the fourth cards.

Push the Aces into the pack, so that all the cards are flush, and then give a false shuffle (see pxii) that retains the top 16 cards on top. Now deal out four hands of four cards, with the last hand coming to you. Show the cards in the first three hands then turn over the cards in your hand – you have got all the Aces!

Tips
This is a good trick to do following any other trick in which the four Aces have been left face up on the table.

Hide and Seek

A Joker and three other cards are sealed in four envelopes which are then mixed up. The envelopes are held briefly behind the performer's back and then one envelope is placed on the table. When it is opened, it is seen to be the one containing the Joker.

Type	Mind-reading
Skill level	Easy
Special techniques	None
Equipment	Pack of cards, four envelopes, a few tiny beads

Preparation
Put the beads in your right jacket pocket. Place the four envelopes and the pack of cards on the table.

Performance
Ask a spectator to take the Joker and three other cards from the pack, to place them on the table, and then to put the pack to one side. As he is doing this, put your right hand into your pocket and slip one of the beads under your thumbnail. Now pick up one of the envelopes and hold it open, with the thumb and forefinger of each hand inside the envelope and your other fingers outside, and ask the spectator to drop the Joker into it. Then ask three other spectators to each pick up one of the remaining envelopes, drop one of the three other cards inside and seal their envelope. As soon as the Joker is in your envelope, rub your right forefinger against your thumbnail so that the bead drops into the envelope, and immediately seal the envelope. Give your envelope to the first spectator and ask him to collect the other envelopes and mix all four of them, so that no one will know which envelope contains the Joker.

Take the four envelopes and hold them behind your back. It is now a simple matter to feel which envelope contains the bead. Bring this envelope forward **45** and place the other three on the table. Hold the envelope you have chosen at one end, between the fingers of your left hand, so that the secret bead drops to the other end. Now take the bottom end of the envelope between the forefinger and thumb of your right hand, pinching the hidden bead between them. Still holding the top end of the envelope with your left hand and retaining the firm grip of your right hand on the bead through the envelope, use your right hand to tear off the bottom of the envelope, so that the Joker falls out onto the table and the bead remains hidden in the torn-off strip.

Immediate Thought

The pack is shuffled by a spectator and is then handed back to the performer. A second spectator is asked to take any card, show it to the audience, and then return it to the pack, which is again shuffled. The spectator's mind is then read by the performer, to discover the identity of the chosen card.

Type	Mind-reading
Skill level	Moderate
Special techniques	Glimpse, false shuffle, force
Equipment	Pack of cards

Performance

Ask a spectator to shuffle the cards and then to hand the pack back to you. Secretly glimpse (see pxxiii) the card at the bottom of the pack and then give the cards a false shuffle (see pxii) to bring the glimpsed card to the top of the pack. Ask a second spectator to take a card but actually force (see pxiii) the top card on him. Tell him to show the card to the audience, without letting you see it, and to return it to the pack, which can then be shuffled. Now pretend to read the spectator's mind and tell him which card he took.

Tips

You will need to use all your acting skills to make this trick effective. Do not announce the name of the card immediately, but instead pretend that a picture of the chosen card is slowly forming in your mind. Say something like 'I'm not completely sure which card it is, but I believe you are thinking of a red card ... I think it is a heart. Yes, it is a heart ... a high card ... but not a picture card. The card you are thinking of is ...' and only then reveal the name of the card.

Impossible Location

One card is chosen by a spectator, and this is returned to the pack. The pack is cut several times and then well shuffled but, impossibly, the chosen card is found by the performer.

Type	Location
Skill level	Advanced
Special techniques	Riffle shuffle
Equipment	Pack of cards

Preparation
Put A♦ on the top of the pack and A♥ on the bottom.

Performance
Place the pack of cards on the table and ask a spectator to take any card. Tell him to look at it, show it to the audience, and then to put it back on top of the pack. Then ask him to cut the cards several times, 'to lose your card somewhere in the pack'. Explain to the audience that a riffle shuffle (see pxi) is the most effective way to mix a pack of cards (this is not true but most people believe that it is) as you cut off about a third of the cards and place them on the bottom of the pack, before dividing the pack into two portions and giving the cards a riffle shuffle.

It seems that the chosen card is now lost but, in fact, it is probably still between the two Aces. Look through the pack with the faces towards you and, if there is one card between the two red Aces, it is the chosen card, which you can reveal in any way that you wish. Sometimes, however, there will be more than one card between the two Aces. What you do next depends upon how many cards there are between the Aces. One way to deal with this is to cut the pack so that the possible cards are at the top and then to hold the pack behind your back. Then take two cards from the bottom of the pack and one card from the top, bring them forward, and ask if the chosen card is one of the three cards. If it is, you will know that it is the one taken from the top of the pack. If the chosen card is not one of these three cards, discard them and take three more cards in the same way until the spectator says that he can see his card. You will then know which card he has chosen, and can reveal its identity with as much drama as you can muster.

Tips
If you know that the spectator is capable of giving the cards a riffle shuffle, you could hand the pack to him and let him perform the shuffle which makes the trick even more impressive.

Insight

A prediction is written on a piece of paper by the performer. The paper is then folded so that no one can see what has been written, and left on the table. A shuffled pack is taken and a portion is cut off, turned face up, and then replaced on the pack by a spectator. A larger batch of cards is then cut off and turned over on the pack. The cards are dealt out and the first (face-down) card is put to one side. The rest of the cards are then dealt onto the table and it is seen that the card the performer predicted is not amongst them. However, when the single face-down card is turned over, it is seen to be the card named at the start by the performer.

Type	Mind-reading
Skill level	Moderate
Special techniques	None
Equipment	Pack of cards, piece of paper, pencil

Performance

Ask a spectator to shuffle the cards and then to hand them back to you. Spread the cards out, face up, between your hands to show that they are well mixed. (What you are really doing is getting sight of the top card which you must remember.) Put the pack on the table, face down, and then pick up the piece of paper and write on it the name of the card you saw at the top of the pack. Fold the piece of paper and leave it in full view on the table.

Ask the spectator to lift off about one-third of the pack, turn it face up and then put it back down on the pack. Now ask him to lift off about two-thirds of the cards, turn them over and put them back down on the pack. If he has followed your instructions correctly (and you will have been watching to make sure that he has), there will be a face-up portion on the top of the pack and the remainder of the cards will be face down.

Now ask the spectator to deal off the top, face-up, cards onto the table one at a time. Tell him to put the first face-down card that he reaches to one side and then to deal the remainder of the pack, face up, on top of those already dealt. When he has finished dealing, all of the pack will be in a face-up pile on the table and there will be one face-down card apart from the rest. Ask the spectator to open up the piece of paper to see what you have written, and then to turn the face-down card over – it is the very card you predicted!

Tips

This version of the trick involves just one spectator, but it is even better if several spectators are part of the trick. So, get one spectator to shuffle the pack, another to make the first cut, a third to make the next cut, someone else to do the dealing, a fifth person to open up the paper and a sixth person to turn over the predicted card. This not only brings more people into the performance but it also makes the trick even more baffling and entertaining.

Instant Identification

A spectator is asked to take any card from a pack that is being held behind the performer's back. Within seconds, the spectator's mind has been read by the performer, who reveals the card chosen by the spectator.

Type	Mind-reading
Skill level	Moderate
Special techniques	Stacked pack, glimpse
Equipment	Pack of cards

Preparation
Stack the pack in the Eight Kings sequence (see pxix).

Performance
Cut the pack a few times (this does not disturb the cyclical sequence of the cards) and then hold them behind your back. Spread the cards between your hands a little and then ask a spectator to take out any card. Emphasize the fact that the spectator must not let you see the card. As you turn back to face the audience, cut the pack at the point from which the card was taken, moving the top half of the pack to the bottom. When you place the pack on the table, tilt the pack a little so that you can glimpse (see pxxiii) the bottom card of the pack. As you know the sequence of the stacked cards, you can work out which card was taken – it will be the card next to the bottom card. So, for example, if the bottom card is K♦, the next card (the card taken) is 3♣. All you now have to do is to employ all your acting skills and announce, in the most mysterious manner possible, the name of the card chosen by the spectator.

Tips
If you return the chosen card to the top of the pack, you can repeat this trick. However, do not perform it more than twice because, sooner or later, someone will ask if they can shuffle the cards and that will destroy your set-up! If someone does insist on shuffling the cards during any trick, allow them to do so and then do a different trick in which the sequence of the cards is irrelevant.

Jumping Jack

Three spectators are asked, in turn, to take a card from the pack, and each card is then placed, face down, on the table. When they are asked to identify their card, each person names the same card – J♥. However, when the chosen cards are turned over, they are seen to be the other three Jacks, for J♥ has vanished from the pack and is found elsewhere.

Type	Transposition
Skill level	Moderate
Special techniques	False shuffle, palm
Equipment	Pack of cards, a half-card (J♥)

Preparation

Take J♥ from a pack of cards similar to the pack you will be using, and cut it in half (see illustration 1 below).

Place one half in your left jacket pocket, and either discard the other half or keep it for some possible future use. In the pack you are going to use for your performance put the intact J♥ somewhere near the centre of the pack and the other three Jacks on the bottom of the pack, and then place the pack in its box.

Performance

Take the pack from its box and give it a false shuffle (see pxii), so that the three Jacks remain on the bottom.

Tell the audience that you are going to take one card from the pack and place it in your pocket as you go through the cards. Then take out the intact J♥ without letting the audience see which card you have taken.

Place the rest of the pack, face down, on the table and ask a spectator to check that your right jacket pocket is empty. While the spectator is examining your pocket, take the opportunity to place your left hand into your left pocket and palm out (see pxxii) the half-card. Then place the intact J♥ into your right pocket (again making sure that the audience do not see the face of the card).

Next pick up the pack with your right hand and place it into your left hand, on top of the palmed half J♥. Now approach a spectator and ask him to look at the bottom card of the pack. You will need to be holding the pack in your left hand, with the half J♥ visible (see illustration 2 opposite).

Then turn your hand downwards and ask the same spectator to pull out the bottom card and place it, face down, on the table. As you are talking to the spectator, bring your right hand against the back of the pack in order to push it forward, towards the spectator's approaching hand. Pushing the pack forward like this causes the whole pack to slide over the half J♥, so that the spectator's fingers come into contact instead with the card next to the half J♥ (one of the other Jacks).

As the spectator places the card he has been tricked into taking face down on the table, square up the pack so that the half J♥ is back in its original position. You now need to repeat the whole procedure for the remaining two Jacks, so that the three Jacks are face down on the table.

Then say to the spectators who have chosen the cards 'I want you all to call out the name of the card you saw.' Naturally, they will all say 'Jack of Hearts'.

Ask them to turn their cards over and, much to everyone's surprise, these are the three other Jacks. While all attention is on the cards being turned, you have plenty of time to palm off the half J♥ into your left hand and drop it into your left pocket.

Finally, ask a spectator to remove the card (the one taken at the beginning of the trick) from your right pocket. It is the missing J♥, the very card each of the spectators had 'seen' in the pack a few moments before!

Tips

It is best to use people who are sitting some distance apart from one another in the audience so that none of them sees which card another spectator looks at.

It is also a good idea to get as close as possible to the spectators choosing the cards, so that other people cannot get a glimpse of the bottom card.

Just a Pinch

The pack is shuffled by a spectator, and a card is taken and shown to the audience, but not to the performer. The pack is then cut into two halves: the chosen card is put on top of one half of the pack, which is then covered by the other half, so that it is lost somewhere in the middle of the pack. The side of the pack is tapped by the performer, and the top half of the pack moves to one side. The cards that have moved are lifted off, and the chosen card is found by the performer at the bottom of this group of cards.

Type	Location
Skill level	Easy
Special techniques	None
Equipment	Pack of cards, salt, empty matchbox

Preparation
Put some salt in the matchbox and then place the matchbox in your pocket.

Performance
Hand a pack of cards to a spectator and ask him to give it a good shuffle. While this is being done, casually put your hand into your pocket, open the matchbox, get some salt on the tip of your forefinger and then close the matchbox. When the spectator has finished shuffling, ask him to put the pack on the table, cut it into two piles, take the top card from one of the piles and show it to the audience. You now point to one of the piles and secretly brush the tip of your forefinger with your thumb, so that some of the salt falls onto the top card, as you say 'Please put your card on top of this half, put the other half on top of that and then square up the pack, so that no one will know where your card is.'

Now tap the side of the pack with the back of your hand and the top part will move. Lift off the cards that have moved and the spectator's card will be at the bottom of that portion.

Tips
The grains of salt act like little rollers to make this trick work and you need only a little salt on your finger to do it. You should experiment to see just how much is needed. If your hands are particularly dry and the salt does not stick to your finger, moisten it by bringing your finger up to your mouth as the spectator is cutting the cards.

Lazy Magician

The performer is feeling tired, so a spectator is asked to do all the work in this trick. A card is chosen, returned to the pack, and then the cards are mixed. A few cards are then turned face up. At this point, the performer wakes up and the card chosen by the spectator is identified by him, even though the cards were not touched by him at any point during the performance.

Type	Mind-reading
Skill level	Easy
Special techniques	None
Equipment	Pack of cards

Performance

Ask a spectator to shuffle the pack and then to take out any eight cards, face down. Tell him to look at the eight cards, choose any one and show it to the audience, then to place it, face down, on top of the pack. Then ask him to put the remaining seven cards, face down, on top of the chosen card, and to cut off about a third of the cards from the top of the pack (the exact number does not matter but it must be more than ten cards). Tell him to take the top card from his packet and to put it to the bottom of the packet, and then to place the next card on the table. Ask him to continue like this through the packet of cards – putting one card to the bottom of the packet, and the next card alongside those already on the table – until all of the cards in the packet are in a row on the table.

As he is doing this, note the position on the table of the fourth card dealt by the spectator, as this is his chosen card. Then ask him to turn the cards face up and to mix them up on the table. This gives you the chance to see the fourth card dealt. All you now have to do is to adopt an expression of the utmost concentration as you read the spectator's mind and then reveal the name of his chosen card.

Lie Detector

The way that polygraph machines ('lie detectors') work is demonstrated by the performer when a chosen card is identified merely by the tone of a spectator's voice.

Type	Location
Skill level	Easy
Special techniques	Glimpse
Equipment	Pack of cards

Performance

Ask a spectator to shuffle the pack of cards and, when he returns the pack to you, glimpse (see pxxiii) the bottom card. Spread the cards, face down, between your hands and ask another spectator to take any card, memorize it, and then place it back on top of the pack. Then cut the pack several times as you talk about the use of polygraph tests (lie detectors) in modern criminology. Tell the audience that these amazing tests actually work by studying the reactions of the suspect and picking up on subtle clues given away during the questioning process. Say that you can do something similar simply by listening to the tone of someone's voice. Then ask the spectator to call out the names of the cards as you deal the pack, face up, on the table and state that you will be able to tell from his voice which card he chose. Deal the cards, one at a time, face up, on the table as the spectator calls out the names of the cards and then stop, with great drama, at the very card the spectator has chosen. You do this not by picking up clues from the tone of his voice, as you have made the audience believe, but by knowing that his chosen card will be the card following the one you memorized earlier.

Tips

Using a known card to locate the position of a chosen card is an important technique in card magic. It can be used in a wide variety of tricks (see, for example, Sure-Fire Bet on p101) and so it is a method well worth developing. Any card that helps locate or keep track of another card or cards in the pack is referred to by magicians as a 'key card'.

Long-Distance Telepathy

The performer having left the room, four cards are removed, by a spectator, from a shuffled pack and these are placed, face up, on the table. One of the four cards is then chosen by another spectator and, on the performer's return to the room, the chosen card is immediately revealed by him.

Type	Mind-reading
Skill level	Moderate
Special techniques	Secret code
Equipment	Pack of cards, a confederate

Preparation

You and your confederate must learn the following two codes and practise the trick. The first code is used to identify any one of four cards – 1 is the lowest card, 2 is the next highest card, 3 is the next highest card and 4 is the highest card in the group. If any of the cards share the same index, then the mnemonic CHaSeD (Clubs, Hearts, Spades, Diamonds) indicates the cards in order of descending value. Thus, the four cards 4♦, 6♥, 9♣, 7♦ would be coded as 1, 2, 4, 3 and the four cards A♣, Q♥, 3♦, Q♣ would be coded as 1, 3, 2, 4 (the Ace counting here as a low card, and Q♣ having a higher value than Q♥).

The second code is based on the position of your confederate's feet (see illustrations below), and is as follows: both feet together = 1; left foot straight and right foot pointing slightly to the right = 2; right foot straight and left foot pointing slightly to the left = 3; feet slightly apart = 4.

Performance

Point to a spectator (your confederate) and ask if he would be willing to take part in a little experiment in telepathy (mind-reading). Explain that you are going to leave the room and, in your absence, you would like him to get four spectators to each take a card from the pack and to lay it, face up, on the table. Then say 'I would like you to think of any one of the four cards. Please take your time and change your mind as many times as you wish. When you have finally decided upon a card, just touch it once, pick up all four cards and mix them together. Then place the cards back on the table, face up, and ask someone to call for me.' You then leave the room and wait until you are called, while the spectator carries out your instructions. When you return to the room, you take a quick, but not too obvious, glance at your confederate's shoes and you will know the code of the chosen card. Pick up the four cards from the table and look at them to work out which card has been chosen. If it makes it easier for you to identify the card, you can always gather your thoughts by sorting the four cards into your code order. Now pretend to concentrate hard as you 'read the spectator's mind', and then announce, with great drama, the name of the card he is thinking of.

Tips

This trick can be repeated, so as to prove your exceptional powers. However, do not do it more than three times or you will end up boring your audience instead of entertaining them. If your confederate wishes to take the part of the performer, you can always swap roles on another occasion.

Look to the Future

The performer's ability to see into the future is showcased: the cards chosen by two spectators are predicted by him.

Type	Mind-reading
Skill level	Moderate
Special techniques	None
Equipment	Pack of cards, cup, two pieces of paper, pencil

Performance

Hand the pack to a spectator and ask him to give the cards a good shuffle and then to return the pack to you. Choose two other spectators, find out their names (let us call them David and Michael) and ask them if they will help you with a little experiment. While you are talking, spread the cards, with the faces towards you, between your hands 'to check that the cards are well mixed' and memorize the card at the bottom of the pack and the card at the top of the pack. Assuming that the two spectators have agreed to help, put down the pack and write on one of the pieces of paper 'David will choose the ...' and write in the name of the card that is at the top of the pack. Fold the slip, without letting anyone see what you have written, and drop it into the cup.

Now approach Michael and say that, while your back is turned, you want him to count a small number of cards from the top of the pack onto the table. When he stops, he has to look at the top card of those dealt, show it to the audience, remember it and then place the pile on the table back on top of the pack. Ask him to give the pack a cut – to bury his card – as you turn back to face the audience and take the pack from him.

As you turn towards David, look through the pack for the card you saw at the bottom of the pack at the start of the trick and cut it to the bottom. Make a mental note of the new top card for that is the card taken by Michael. Hand the pack to David and ask him to do exactly the same as Michael did – count down the same number of cards, look at and remember the last card dealt, show it to the audience, and then cut it into the pack. If he has forgotten the number of cards Michael dealt, he can ask Michael to whisper the number to him. Before David does all this, pick up the second piece of paper and write on it 'Michael will choose the ...', and write in the name of the card you have just seen on top of the pack. Then fold the piece of paper and drop it into the cup.

Ask both spectators for the names of the cards they have chosen, as you pick up the cup and tip the two pieces of paper into your hand, immediately passing them to someone else to open. When the pieces of paper are opened, it appears that you really have foretold the future.

Tips
While it is essential for this trick, it is always good practice to ask for the name of any person who helps you with a trick. This personalizes the trick and makes it more memorable for those involved.

Lost and Found

Some cards are dealt out by a spectator, a card is chosen and this is then cut into the pack. The chosen card is then brought to either the top or the bottom of the pack by the performer.

Type	Location
Skill level	Moderate
Special techniques	None
Equipment	Pack of cards

Performance

Ask a spectator to shuffle the cards and then to hand them back to you. Spread the cards out, face up, to show the audience that they are well mixed. What you are really doing, however, is identifying the top and bottom cards. Then close up the pack and place it, face down, on the table.

Now ask another spectator to deal cards, from the top of the pack, onto the table and to stop dealing whenever he wants. Then ask him to look at the top card of either the pile on the table or of the cards he still holds, to remember it and also to show it to the audience. Ask him to put this card on top of either of the two packets and then to put the other packet on top of this, so that his card is lost somewhere in the pack. Tell him that he can cut the pack a few times if he wishes, so that no one knows the location of his card.

Now take the cards and look through them until you see one of the cards you noted earlier. Put the card which is to the right of this card on the bottom of the pack. Continue to go through the cards until you see the second card you noted and, this time, put the card which is to the right of this card on the top of the pack. Remember which card is on the top and which card is on the bottom of the pack. Now put the pack, face down, on the table as you tell the audience that you have found the spectator's card.

Ask the spectator for the name of the card he chose. If it is the top card of the pack, simply turn it over to show that you have found it. If it is the bottom card of the pack, just turn the whole pack over, to show that you have, once again, accomplished the impossible.

Lucky Seven

A pile of cards chosen by a spectator is predicted by the performer.

Type	Mind-reading
Skill level	Easy
Special techniques	None
Equipment	Pack of cards, paper, pencil

Performance

Without letting the audience see which cards you are removing, go through the pack and take out the four sevens and place them, face down, in a pile on the table. Now take any seven cards (try not to make it obvious how many cards you are taking) and place them on the table in another pile, face down. Then make a third pile of just three cards – an Ace, a two and a four – and place them, face down, in a pile alongside the other two piles.

Next, take the piece of paper and write on it 'You will choose the seven pile.' Fold the paper, without letting the audience see what you have written, and put it on the table.

Now ask a spectator to point to any one of the three piles. Tell him that he has a perfectly free choice and that he can even change his mind if he wants to. Once he has chosen a pile, pick up the other two piles and place them back on the pack.

Now ask another spectator to unfold, and read, the piece of paper. You then pick up the chosen pile, to show that you have correctly foretold the future. Your prediction will be correct, no matter which pile is chosen. If the four sevens are chosen simply turn over the cards to show them; if the pile of seven cards is chosen, count the cards in the pile; and, if the third pile is chosen, turn them over to show that the values add up to seven.

you will choose
the
seven pile

Make a Call

After a card is chosen by a spectator, the performer telephones a friend and is told the name of the chosen card.

Type	Mind-reading
Skill level	Easy
Special techniques	Break control
Equipment	Pack of cards, a confederate

Performance

Ask a spectator to shuffle the cards and then to hand the pack back to you. Spread the cards, face down, and ask a second spectator to take any card and to show it to the audience. As he is doing this, lift off about half of the cards and ask the spectator to place the chosen card on the lower portion of the pack, and then drop the remainder of the pack on top of this. Cut the pack a few times, using the break control (see pxxii) to bring the chosen card to the top of the pack. Now say to the spectator 'The cards are well mixed and your card is lost somewhere in the pack.' Casually spread out the cards with their faces towards you, so that you can quickly glance at the top (chosen) card. Then close up the cards and hand them to another spectator, as you say 'But perhaps you would like to shuffle them to make sure?'

It is important that you remember the chosen card, for you now have to pass on that information to the friend whom you are about to telephone, without the audience being aware that this is what you are doing.

Tell the audience that you have a friend with amazing telepathic powers, who will probably know which card has been chosen, and that you will call him to find out. Then telephone your friend, who is waiting for your call. When he answers, he says in a whisper, leaving a pause between each of the suits, 'Clubs, Hearts, Spades, Diamonds'. You say 'Hello, is Mark (or whatever his name is) there?' as soon as he names the correct suit. Your friend now knows the suit of the chosen card, so he then starts counting very quietly, from Ace to King. As soon as he reaches the value of the chosen card, you say 'Hi, Mark. I have a call for you.' As your friend now knows the identity of the chosen card, you hand the telephone to the spectator who chose the card and your friend tells him which card he chose!

Mental Spell

A card is chosen by a spectator and its name is spelled out by him, moving one card for each letter. The next card turned over by the performer is the very card chosen by the spectator.

Type	Location
Skill level	Moderate
Special techniques	False shuffle
Equipment	Pack of cards

Preparation

Arrange three sets of five cards as follows: A♣, 5♣, 4♥, 3♠, J♦; 10♣, A♥, J♠, 8♥, 9♦; and 2♣, 6♠, 5♥, 7♠, 4♦. Note that the first card in each group (eg Ace of Clubs) is spelled with ten letters, the second with eleven letters, the third with twelve, the fourth with 13 and the last one in each group with 14. Put these cards on top of the pack.

Performance

Give the pack a false shuffle (see pxii), so that the 15 cards you placed on top of the pack remain undisturbed. Now draw off five cards and, keeping them in the same order, put them in a pile on the table. Draw off two more sets of five cards and place them in two piles alongside the first. Try not to make it obvious that you are counting the cards as you do this. Ask a spectator to pick any one of the three piles. Pick up the chosen pile, show the faces of the cards to the spectator and ask him to concentrate on any one of the cards he sees. When he has chosen one, put the cards back on the pack and then pick up the other two piles and place them on the top of the pack. Give the cards a false shuffle, retaining these 15 cards on the top and place the pack on the table.

Now ask the spectator to spell out the name of his card, by taking one card for each letter (including the word 'of') from the top of the pack. Then turn over the next card, and it is his chosen card!

Tips

It is a good idea to get the spectator to whisper the name of his card to another spectator, so that you do not have to worry about the possibility of his forgetting which card he has chosen.

Mind Control

A spectator is asked to concentrate on any one card in a batch of cards. The cards are mixed up and dealt out again, face down. The spectator is then offered a series of blind choices and he unfailingly finds his own chosen card.

Type	Mind-reading
Skill level	Moderate
Special techniques	None
Equipment	Pack of cards

Performance

Deal out four piles each containing eight cards and ask a spectator to choose any pile. Pick up the chosen pile with four cards, fanned out face down, in each hand. Then tell the spectator that you are going to ask him to think of any one of the cards that you are holding. Lift both of your hands simultaneously, showing the cards briefly to the spectator and the audience and, after just a second, lower them again. In that instant, you will be able to see from the spectator's eye movement which hand he is looking at. You then place that group of cards underneath the four cards you are holding in your other hand. Pick up one of the other piles of eight cards from the table and put it on top of the eight cards you are now holding in your hand, and then drop these cards on top of the other two piles remaining on the table.

Now deal the 32 cards out into four piles. Show the cards in each pile to the spectator and ask him which pile contains his card. Discard the other three piles and deal the eight cards in the last remaining pile, face down, into two rows of four cards. The card selected by the spectator will always be the one in the lower left-hand corner and you must now make sure that the spectator chooses that card.

Ask the spectator if he would like to pick the top or the bottom row of cards. If he says 'the bottom row', say 'OK, we will use them' and you gather up the top row of cards and place them on the pack. If he says 'the top row' gather them up as you say 'OK, we will get rid of them'. Either way, the top row of cards is discarded and the bottom row is left on the table.

Now ask the spectator to touch two cards. If one of the cards he touches is the chosen card, simply pick up the untouched ones and put them back on the pack. If neither of the cards he touches is the chosen card, take both of them and place them on the pack. You are now left with two cards, one of which is the chosen card.

Tell the spectator to pick up either card. If he picks up the chosen card, take the other card and place it on the pack, then ask him to turn over the card he is holding – and it will be his chosen card. If he picks up the other card, you say 'Please put it back on the pack'. This leaves the chosen card on the table, for you to turn over as dramatically as you can.

Tips
The final 'choice' of card is known to magicians as 'equivoque': the clever interpretation by the performer of the spectator's selection in either a negative or positive way, to ensure that a card or object is forced upon the spectator. It is a useful technique as it can be used in many different situations.

Mismatched

The outcome of a random mixing of the cards is predicted by the performer.

Type	Mind-reading
Skill level	Moderate
Special techniques	Palm
Equipment	Pack of cards, two small pieces of paper, pencil

Preparation
Secretly put two red cards from the pack you will be using into your pocket.

Performance
Ask a spectator to shuffle the cards and, while he is doing this, explain to the audience that you are going to have the cards placed down in a random manner but that you will still be able to predict the outcome.

When the spectator has finished shuffling the cards, ask him if he would like the red cards or the black cards. If he chooses the red cards, write on the first slip of paper 'Your pile will contain two fewer cards than mine.' If he chooses the black cards, write instead 'My pile will contain two fewer cards than yours.' Then fold the slip of paper, so that no one can see what you have written, and leave it on the table.

Now ask the spectator to deal out the cards, face up, in pairs of like colour. If two reds are dealt together, they go onto a 'red' pile; if two blacks are dealt together, they go on a 'black' pile; and, if the pairs are of different colours, they are put on a 'discard' pile.

When all the cards have been dealt, ask the spectator to count the cards in the pile of his chosen colour, and then to count the cards in your pile. Finally, ask him to open your prediction and read it out, and it is seen to be correct!

While the spectator is counting the cards, you casually put your hand into your pocket and palm out (see pxxii) the two cards placed there earlier. You then pick up the discard pile and secretly add these two cards to it. The audience will not notice what you are doing as all their attention will be focused on the cards being counted and the prediction being opened.

Once the prediction has been read, gather all the cards together as if the trick has finished. Hand the pack to another spectator and ask him to give the cards a good shuffle. As this is being done, write on the second slip of paper 'We will both have the same number of cards.' You now go through the same procedure as before, with the spectator putting red pairs and black pairs in two separate piles, and the mixed pairs to one side.

When the red and black piles are counted, you ask the spectator to open and read out your prediction on the second slip of paper. You are correct once again!

Tips

Do not draw attention to yourself when you palm the cards from your pocket. At that point, all attention will be on the spectator counting the cards and revealing the prediction, so simply pick up the discard pile, square up the packet of cards and add the palmed cards at the same time. When the spectator has finished counting, take the rest of the cards from the table and add them to the cards you are holding.

Mission Impossible

The pack is shuffled by a spectator and is handed to the performer. The cards are spread out, face down, and a second spectator is asked to take a card and then to return it to the pack. A third spectator is asked to think of a number and, while the performer turns his back, to deal that number of cards onto the table and then to put the dealt cards back on top of the pack. The cards are then shuffled by the performer, who is once again facing the audience. The number chosen by the third spectator is then used to determine the number of cards dealt out. Much to everyone's surprise, the chosen card is also at that number.

Type	Mind-reading
Skill level	Advanced
Special techniques	Break control, false shuffle
Equipment	Pack of cards

Performance

Ask a spectator to shuffle the cards and then to hand the pack back to you. Spread out the cards, face down, and ask a second spectator to take any card, show it to the audience and then to replace it in the pack. Cut the cards a few times but in fact perform the break control (see pxxii) to bring the chosen card to the top of the pack.

Turn to a third spectator and ask him to think of any number between 5 and 20. Hold the pack in your left hand and, while you are talking, secretly push the top card a little to the right, digging your right thumbnail into the corner of the top card, and then push the card back on top of the pack. Say to the third spectator 'To allow the audience to know which number you have chosen, will you please deal off that number of cards from the top of the pack onto the table, then pick them up and put them back on top of the pack. Please deal as quietly as possible so that I will not know your number. I will turn my back for a moment so that I cannot see what you are doing. Please tell me when you have finished.'

Turn away until the spectator has finished. When you turn back, take the pack and give it a false shuffle (see pxii) that keeps the top 20 or so cards still on the top of the pack. Then, start dealing cards, from the top of the pack, onto the table. With your right forefinger touching the face of each card as you deal, you will be able to feel the card with the nick made by your thumbnail when you reach it. This will be at the same position in the pack as the number of cards the spectator is thinking of. Keep the last card in your right hand as you say 'You may be wondering how I knew your number. That was easy because the card chosen by this gentleman (the second spectator) is at that number in the pack.' Turn to the second spectator and ask him for the name of his card. Accept your applause as you turn over the card in your hand, which is the spectator's card!

Move It

A spectator is asked to think of any card in the pack. Another spectator is then requested to count back from the bottom of the pack to the chosen card, to remember the number of cards counted, and then to cut the pack several times. The cards are then taken by the performer and are held behind his back. The chosen card (not known to the performer) is then shown to have moved to another position in the pack.

Type	Skill demonstration
Skill level	Moderate
Special techniques	Crimp
Equipment	Pack of cards

Performance

Ask a spectator to think of any card in the pack and then to whisper it to another spectator. As you are talking, put a crimp (see pxxiii) in the corner of the card second from the top of the pack and then hand the pack to the second spectator. Ask him to count back from the bottom of the pack to the card chosen by the first spectator, and to remember that number. Then tell him to cut the cards several times and to hand the pack back to you.

Take the cards behind your back and cut the pack, in order to bring the crimped card to the top. Now take seven cards from the top of the pack (straightening out the crimp as you do so) and place them on the bottom of the pack, before bringing the pack forward and placing it on the table.

Ask the second spectator for the position from the bottom of the pack of the first spectator's chosen card. Whatever the reply, you say something like 'That's interesting, for I have just moved it to such-and-such a position.' When naming the position, make the number eight higher than the number the spectator has just said. So, if the spectator says '17', you say '25'; if the spectator says '20', you say '28'. Ask the first spectator for the name of the card he is thinking of and then ask a third spectator to count from the bottom of the pack to the number you have just given and there, sure enough, is the first spectator's card.

Tips

The easiest way to get a crimp in the card second from the top is to spread the cards with their faces towards the audience, to show they are well mixed. Spread the two top cards wider than the ones below them so that your left thumb can push against the bottom-left corner of the second card to bend it. You will find another use for this technique in Touch of Magic (see p109).

Nonsensical Formula

The pack is shuffled by a spectator and is then divided into two portions, the spectator having one portion and the performer the other. The cards in each portion are counted and the spectator is asked to move the cards, following the performer's example, resulting in the spectator and the performer both having one card in each of their pockets. The card in the performer's right pocket is removed and, after performing a complicated mathematical calculation, the card in the spectator's right pocket is identified. Using the same mathematical calculation, the card in the performer's left pocket is used to identify the card in the spectator's left pocket.

Type	Mind-reading
Skill level	Moderate
Special techniques	None
Equipment	Pack of cards

Performance

Ask a spectator to shuffle the cards, then take them back and fan them out, face up, 'to show that they are well mixed'. As you are doing this, look at, and remember, the third and fourth cards from the bottom of the pack. Close up the cards and place the pack, face down, on the table. Then, ask the spectator to lift off a portion of the cards and to place them on the table. Ask him to point to either one of the portions. If he points to what was the upper part of the pack, say 'OK, I'll have this portion and you have the other one.' If he points to what was the lower part of the pack, say 'OK, you take this portion and I'll take the other one.' Either way, the spectator ends up with the lower portion of the pack.

Each of you now deals your own portion of the pack onto the table and counts the number of cards in it. (The purpose of this is not really to count the cards, but to bring the memorized cards to the third and fourth position from the top of the pack.) If the spectator ends up with an even number of cards, say 'Oh, I need you to have an odd number of cards for this trick.' Then take one card from the top of his portion and put it on top of your portion. If he has an odd number of cards, say 'Oh, I need you to have an even number of cards for this trick.' Then take one card from the top of his portion and put it on top of your portion.

Now ask the spectator to follow your moves exactly. Take one card from the bottom of your portion and push it into the middle of the cards you hold, and then take one card from the top of your portion and also push this into the middle of your portion. Next take the top card and place it, unseen, into your right coat pocket. Then take a card from the bottom of the pack and push it into the middle of the cards and then take one card from the top and place it, again unseen, into your left pocket. The situation now is that the spectator has what was originally the card third from the bottom of the pack in his right pocket and the card that was originally fourth from the bottom in his left pocket.

Take the card from your right pocket and say 'This is ... (whatever the card is) which has a co-efficient factor of 2456 which multiplied by pi squared and then divided by the resultant logarithm means that the card in your right pocket must have a co-efficient factor of 4876, so the card in your right pocket is ...' (and you name the card which was third from the bottom at the start of the trick). Then take the card from your left pocket, name it and then spout another nonsense formula before identifying the card in the spectator's left pocket (which was the fourth card from the bottom at the start).

Numbered Thoughts

While the performer has his back turned, a spectator is asked to think of a number between 10 and 20. He is then told to deal, silently, that number of cards from the pack and to remember the card reached at the chosen number. The pack is then cut several times by the spectator. The cards are taken by the performer, now facing the audience, who reveals how many cards were counted by the spectator and which card was selected.

Type	Mind-reading
Skill level	Moderate
Special techniques	Complete cut
Equipment	Pack of cards

Preparation
Put two known cards (say, the two red Aces) at the top and the bottom of the pack.

Performance
Ask a spectator to think of any number between 10 and 20, to silently deal that number of cards from the pack and to remember the card at the chosen number. Turn away from the audience while he doing this. Now ask the spectator to place the rest of the pack on top of the cards he has dealt and then to give the pack several complete cuts (see pxv). Now turn back round to face the audience and take the pack. Casually look at the card faces as you talk about the impossibility of your knowing which card has been chosen. What you are doing at this point is looking for the cards you placed at the top and bottom of the pack earlier. The number of cards between your two known cards, including the first but not the second known card, is the number

chosen by the spectator, and the card to the right of the second of your two cards is the card memorized by the spectator. So, you can now pretend to read his mind and tell him the number of cards he took and the name of his chosen card.

Tips
Once you are feeling more confident as a performer, you can decide not to prepare the pack in advance, but simply to look quickly at the cards at the beginning of your performance, memorizing the top and bottom cards.

Observation Test

The pack of cards is shuffled by a spectator and is then returned to the performer. The cards are spread out, face down, and a second spectator is asked to take a card, look at it, and then to replace it in the pack. The four Aces are shown to the audience and the spectator is asked to take part in an observation test involving the Aces. However, the spectator's powers of perception fail him, for the last card is magically transformed into his original chosen card.

Type	Transformation
Skill level	Moderate
Special techniques	Break control, false shuffle, glide
Equipment	Pack of cards

Performance
Ask a spectator to shuffle the cards and then to hand them back to you. Spread the cards, face down, between your hands and ask a second spectator to take any card, show it to the audience, and then return it to the pack. Next secretly bring the chosen card to the top of the pack using the break control (see pxxii) or any other method, and then false shuffle (see pxii) it to the bottom of the pack. Spread the cards, with the faces towards you, and openly take out the four Aces and put them on the very bottom of the pack, beneath the chosen card (being careful not to let the audience see the chosen card). Position the two black Aces between the two reds, so that the order from the bottom of the pack is red Ace, black Ace, black Ace, red Ace, chosen card.

Now take the Aces from the pack into your right hand, but actually take the chosen card as well (although the audience must not, of course, be aware of this), and place the rest of the pack to one side. Transfer the four (really five) cards to your left hand in readiness for the glide (see pxx). Say that you are now going to test the audience's powers of observation as you show the red Ace on the bottom of the packet you are holding. Turn your hand over, draw out the bottom card and place it, face up, on the table as you say 'red'. Show the next card (a black Ace), turn your hand over, pull out the bottom card and place it face up on top of the first Ace, saying 'black'. For the next move, do not show the bottom card, perform the glide and take the top two cards in your right hand (being careful to keep them together for the audience must believe that you have only one card in your hand). Place them, face up, as one card, on the other two Aces, saying 'red'. You now have just one card in your left hand (a black Ace). Take it in your right hand and place it, face up, on top of the other Aces, saying 'black'.

Pick up the Aces (and the hidden card) and hold them, face down, in readiness for the glide, as you say 'I expect that you have noticed that the colours alternate but, in case you didn't see this, I'll show you the cards again.' Then, perform exactly the same moves as before, until you have one card remaining in your left hand. This time, though, the first bottom card that you draw out and place, face up, on the table will be a black Ace. It will be followed by a red Ace. As before, you then perform the glide and place the two top cards (as one), face up, on top of the others, to show a black Ace. This leaves one card in your left hand which you put, face down, on the table away from the other cards.

Then pick up the pile of Aces and place it back on the main part of the pack, as you say, pointing to the separate face-down card, 'I showed you that the colours alternate but I wonder how many of you were watching closely enough to know the suit of this card?' Then casually cut the pack to lose the Aces somewhere in the middle. When a member of the audience answers your question, say 'Ah, but did you notice its value?' They will reply 'It was an Ace.'

Ask for the name of the card that was chosen at the start of the trick and then turn over the face-down card to show that it is the chosen card, not the Ace that everyone expected.

On the Move

A black card is made to jump to different places in a packet of red cards.

Type	Transposition
Skill level	Moderate
Special techniques	None
Equipment	Pack of cards, a special card

Preparation

Take two cards – one red and one black – from a pack with the same back design as the pack you are going to use. Cut 0.5mm from one end of the red card, and apply some glue to the back of this card, just above the cut edge. Press it down on top of the (face-up) black card, so that the bottom edges of both cards are flush (see illustration 1 below). Place the genuine black card on the bottom of the pack, and place next to it (second from the bottom) the special card.

①

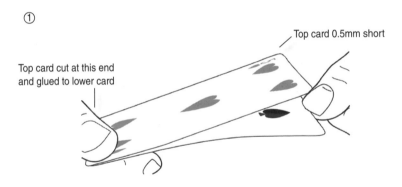

Top card cut at this end and glued to lower card

Top card 0.5mm short

Performance

Hold the pack face up and deal the black card onto the table. Then deal off ten red cards as you come to them, the first being the special card. Pick up all the reds, turn them face down, and place the genuine black card, face down, on top of the packet.

Place the forefinger of your right hand against the end of the top (black) card and lift it a little to show it to the audience (see illustration 2 overleaf).

②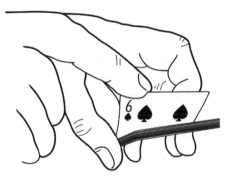

Then take this card from the top of the packet and put it underneath the special card so that it is second from the top of the packet. Now use your forefinger, as before, to lift the end of the top card. As the red card that forms part of the special card has been shortened, the audience will see the black card and so it seems that the black card has jumped back to the top of the packet.

Again, take the top (special) card and place it second from the top of the packet. Lift up the end of the top card, as before, and it seems that the black card has jumped to the top again. Slowly, take the top card (ie the single black card) and place it on the bottom of the packet. Lift the front end again to show that the black has again returned to the top.

Now take the top (special) card and place it in the middle of the packet. Slowly turn over the whole packet and, to everyone's amazement, the black card is now on the bottom! Say laughingly 'I can never keep up with that black card!' as you deal all the cards in the packet, face up, onto the pack, thus showing that there is only one black card amongst the reds (but without actually saying so).

One Good Turn

A spectator is invited to take half of the pack and to hand the other half to the performer. While the performer has his back to the audience, the spectator is asked to take one card from his portion of the pack, to show it to the audience and then to put it, face down, on top of the cards he is holding. The performer turns back round to face the audience and his portion of the pack is placed, in turn, on top of the spectator's card. The cards are then held behind the spectator's back and one card is inserted, face up, in the pack. When the cards are spread out, it is seen that the spectator has put the face-up card next to the card chosen earlier.

Type	Location
Skill level	Easy
Special techniques	None
Equipment	Pack of cards

Performance

Ask a spectator to shuffle the cards and then to give you about half of the pack. Turn away from the audience as you ask him to take any card from his half of the pack, to show it to the audience and then to put it, face down, on top of the cards he is holding. While he is doing this, secretly turn the bottom card of your cards face up and the second card from the top face up as well. Turn back to face the audience and put your cards on top of the cards the spectator is holding. Ask him to hold the cards behind his back, then to take the top card from the pack and to put it on the bottom of the pack. Tell him to take the next top card, turn it over, push it into the pack at any point, and then to place the pack on the table. Spread the cards out until a face-up card becomes visible. Then ask the spectator which card he chose and turn over the card to the left of the face-up card. It is the spectator's card, and so you can congratulate him on finding the card himself!

Tips

Occasionally the spectator may put the top card between the face-up card and his chosen card. If this happens, the card you turn over will not be the card chosen by the spectator, so you say 'You missed it by one!' Then you turn over the next card (which will be the spectator's card) and continue 'But that's not at all bad for a beginner.'

Order, Order

Thirteen cards of the same suit, all in numerical order, are shown to the audience by the performer. The cards are then dealt according to a spectator's instructions. No matter how the cards are mixed, the performer's magical skills are employed to keep the cards in the same order as at the outset.

Type	Transposition
Skill level	Easy
Special techniques	None
Equipment	Pack of cards

Performance

Take out the 13 cards of one suit and show them to the audience in numerical order, from Ace to King (see illustration below).

Put the rest of the pack to one side. Turn the 13 cards face down and tell a spectator that you will deal cards on the table according to his instructions. If he says 'single', you will deal one card and, if he says 'double', you will take the top card, place it beneath the next card and deal both cards together.

Then go through the packet, doing exactly what the spectator asks. Pick up the 13 cards and say 'We will do that again, just to make sure that the cards are well mixed.' Repeat the process, once again following the instructions given to you by the spectator: on the word 'single', deal a single card, and on the word 'double', put the top card beneath the next card and deal both of them together.

Now tell the audience that you have such power over the cards that, even though they have been thoroughly mixed, your magic can put them back in the correct order. Spread out the cards, face up, and let everyone see that they are in the correct numerical order, as they were at the beginning!

Tips
Although this trick works automatically, do not let the audience know this. Let them think that the cards are in order because of your magical powers.

Out for the Count

A card, chosen by a spectator, is shown to the rest of the audience, and is then shuffled back into the pack. Some cards are then dealt by the spectator onto the performer's hand. The last card dealt is shown to be the very same one the spectator chose earlier.

Type	Location
Skill level	Advanced
Special techniques	Force, palm
Equipment	Pack of cards, one extra card

Preparation
Take one card from another pack similar to the one you will be using. Put this card in your right pocket.

Performance
Run through the pack with the faces towards you and move the duplicate of the card in your pocket (let us say that it is 6♥) and put it on the top of the pack. Ask a spectator to choose a card but actually force (see pxiii) 6♥. Ask him to look at the card, remember it, show it to the audience then push it back into the pack.

Shuffle the cards and then hand the pack to the spectator, saying 'Perhaps you would prefer to shuffle the cards yourself?' While he is shuffling the cards, casually put your hand into your pocket and palm out (see pxxii) the duplicate card.

Now ask the spectator to deal cards, one at a time, from the top of the pack and onto your outstretched left hand. After he has dealt five or six cards, say 'Stop dealing whenever you like.' Then add, jokingly, 'Sooner rather than later!' When he stops dealing, look directly at him and say 'You will agree that you had a perfectly free choice of card?' (Actually, he didn't, but he doesn't know that.) Then say 'And you decided when to stop dealing?' Of course, he will agree with you. While you are talking, you place the palmed card on top of those in your left hand. Stretch out your left hand towards him, ask him which card he chose and get him to look at the card he stopped at. Enjoy the look of astonishment on his face when he sees that it is his chosen card!

Tips

At the end of this trick, you have two cards of the same value in the pack and you must get rid of one of them before proceeding with other tricks. The easiest way to do this is to put the cards into the box and, the next time you use them, to leave the duplicate card in it.

Another method is to leave the chosen card on top of the pack and palm it away and back into your pocket when you have the opportunity. However, do not do this straight away for someone will spot it. Take your time and do it while attention is elsewhere.

Outnumbered

A card is chosen by a spectator and is returned to the pack. The spectator selects any number from 1 to 52 but when the performer counts down to that number it is not the chosen card. The pack is reassembled and the spectator counts down to his selected number. The last card dealt is his chosen card.

Type	Location
Skill level	Moderate
Special techniques	False shuffle or false cut
Equipment	Pack of cards

Performance

Ask someone in your audience to shuffle the pack. Take the pack back and spread out the cards, face down, and ask a spectator to take any card and show it to the rest of the audience. Lift off some of the cards for the chosen card to be replaced in the middle of the pack. You then perform either a false shuffle (see pxii) or a false cut (see pxvii) so that the chosen card is secretly brought to the top of the pack.

Now ask a spectator for any number from 1 to 52. Deal the chosen number of cards from the top of the pack onto the table. (Unbeknown to the audience the first card dealt is the chosen card.) When you reach the selected number, turn the next card over and act surprised that it is not the selected card.

Pick up the dealt cards and put them back on top of the pack as you suggest that the trick could be more successful if a spectator did the counting. Ask the spectator to deal the cards, one at a time, onto the table, until the selected number is reached. Ask him to turn that card face up and get the rest of the audience to applaud as the card being shown is the very one selected earlier.

Over Easy

A spectator is asked to take any card from the pack. The card is shown to the audience and is then pushed back into the pack at any point. While the pack is held briefly behind the performer's back, one card is reversed. When the pack is brought forward and spread out on the table, the reversed card is revealed to be the card selected by the spectator.

Type	Location
Skill level	Moderate
Special techniques	Ribbon spread
Equipment	Pack of cards

Preparation
Secretly turn the bottom card of the pack face up and put the pack back into its box.

Performance
Take the pack from its box and spread the cards out, face down, between your hands. Be careful not to expose the reversed card at the bottom of the pack. Ask a spectator to take out any card and to show it to the audience. As he is showing the card to the audience, close up the spread of cards and then discreetly turn the whole pack upside down.

Ask the spectator to push his card, face down, anywhere in the pack. Be careful not to let anyone see that all the cards, except one, are actually face up. Then tell the audience that you are going to find the spectator's card with the pack held behind your back. Hold the pack behind your back, in your left hand, push the top (secretly-reversed) card into your right hand and then turn the whole pack over on top of this card.

Then bring the pack back to the front and ribbon spread (see pxix) the cards, face down, across the table. Somewhere in the middle of the pack there will be one face-up card – the card that the spectator chose earlier.

People Power

Two spectators are seated on opposite sides of a table, with the performer standing at the head of the table between them. The spectator on the performer's left is asked to shuffle the pack of cards and to place it on the performer's left hand. The spectator on the performer's right is then asked to cut off a portion of cards and place them on the table in front of himself. The remainder of the pack is then placed in front of the person on the performer's left. Each spectator is asked to take five cards from the top of his part of the pack and to place them, face down, on the table. Each then chooses, and memorizes, one of his five cards, which is then pushed, face down, into the other spectator's group of five cards. The packets of cards are then mixed up. The five cards to his left are taken by the performer, and one card is removed by him. It is found to be the one chosen by the person on his right. The same procedure is followed with the other packet of cards. Again, the card taken by the performer is found to be the one chosen by the other spectator.

Type	Mind-reading
Skill level	Moderate
Special techniques	Palm
Equipment	Pack of cards, safety pin, paper clip

Preparation

Make a card clip out of a safety pin and a paper clip (see p6). Take five playing cards from the pack and memorize them, before placing them in the clip which is attached to the back lining of your jacket.

Performance

Invite two spectators to come up and sit on either side of your table (we will call the spectator to your left 'A' and the spectator to your right 'B'). Remove the pack from its box and hand it to A, asking him to give the cards a good shuffle and then to place the pack, face down, on your open left palm.

You then turn to B and ask him to cut off about half of the cards and put them on the table in front of him. While this is being done, you slip your right hand beneath your jacket and secretly pull the five cards from the clip into your right palm (see pxxii).

You now swing back to your left, to speak to A and, as you do so, your two hands come together for a second so that you can drop the palmed cards on top of the half-pack on your left hand. Put the half-pack in front of A and ask both spectators to take five cards from the top of the pack in front of them and to place them, face down, on the table. Take a step backwards away from the table as you ask each of them to take any one card from their five cards, look at it and memorize it. Suggest that they each show their chosen card to the audience and then ask them to place it in the other person's set of cards. Then tell them to mix up the five cards they now hold and to put them, face down, on the table.

You now step back towards the table, and stress to the audience how difficult it is for anyone to find the memorized cards. Tell them that you will, in fact, have to use your superhuman mental powers to do so. Pick up the five cards in front of A and look through them – four of them will be from your memorized set and the odd one out will be B's card. Take it out and show it to B, so that he can confirm that it is his chosen card. Now pick up the five cards in front of B and look for the last of your five memorized cards, which you can then reveal, to thunderous applause, as A's card.

Tips
If you always use the same five cards for this trick, it will save you memorizing a new set every time. If you wish to perform this trick but you do not have the card clip available, simply put the five cards into your right-hand pocket and palm them out from there.

Piano Trick

Pairs of cards are placed between a spectator's fingers by the performer. The cards are then removed and divided up into two piles. Magically, one card is transferred from one pile to the other.

Type	Transposition
Skill level	Easy
Special techniques	None
Equipment	Pack of cards

Performance
Ask a spectator to place both of his hands on the table. You then lift up his wrists, so that his fingertips are left resting, arched, on the table top, like someone playing the piano (hence the title of this trick). Take two cards and say 'two cards, an even number', as you place them in the gap between the little finger and third finger of the spectator's right hand, with one long edge of the cards resting on the table top. Then ask him to close his fingers in order to hold them in place (see illustration 1 overleaf).

Take two more cards as you say 'two more cards, even' and put them between the spectator's middle and third fingers. Again say 'two cards, always a pair, always even', as you put two cards between his forefinger and middle finger. You then place a final pair of cards between his thumb and forefinger. Do exactly the same with his left hand, laying emphasis on the word 'even' as before but, this time, put just one card between his thumb and forefinger as you say 'one card, odd' (see illustration 2 below).

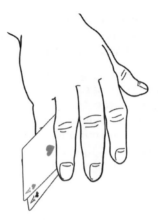

Single 'odd' card

Pause for a moment before you continue. Take one pair of cards from the spectator and lay the two cards, face down, alongside one another as you say 'two cards, a pair, even'. Take a second pair and place one card on each of the two cards on the table, again saying 'two cards, a pair, even'. Continue taking pairs of cards and laying one card of each pair on each of the piles on the table, each time reiterating the mantra 'two cards, a pair, even'. When you have dealt with all of the pairs in this manner, take the single card from between the spectator's thumb and forefinger and ask him 'On which of these two even piles shall I put this odd card?' The card is placed on the pile chosen by the spectator which, you say, now makes that even pile an odd pile. You now announce that you will cause that odd card to fly magically to the other pile. Then wave your hands in a mysterious fashion over the two piles, as if magically transferring the card from one pile to the other. Take the pile to which the odd card was added and remove cards in pairs. Say something like 'even pair, even pair, even pair...', and the pairs come out even. You then do exactly the same with the other pile and you are left with one odd card – which must have travelled from the other pile!

Tips

The success of this trick depends to a great extent on the repetition of the word 'even' as the pairs are formed throughout the performance and it is a good example of how a performer can misdirect the attention of the audience by the use of words. It has been performed by magicians for over a hundred years!

Pocket It

The pack is shuffled by a spectator, a card is memorized and its position from the top of the pack is noted. One card is removed from the pack by the performer, and this is then placed in his pocket. The position of the memorized card is then revealed to the audience by the spectator. However, on counting down to that number, it is found that the card has disappeared. The spectator is asked to take the card from the performer's pocket. To everyone's amazement, it is the memorized card.

Type	Mind-reading
Skill level	Advanced
Special techniques	Palm
Equipment	Pack of cards

Performance

Ask a spectator to shuffle the pack and to choose, and memorize, any card in the top half of the pack. Then ask him to work out, and remember (but not to tell you), its position from the top of the pack. Now tell the audience that you are going to remove one card from the pack. Take the pack behind your back and, with your right hand, take out any card near the bottom of the pack and place it in your right pocket, being careful not to let anyone see which card it is. What you actually do is place the card in your pocket and immediately palm it out again (see pxxii), as your left hand brings the pack forward into view. You then return the card to the top of the pack, as you move the pack casually from your left hand to your right hand.

Now say to the audience that you wish to confirm the spectator's choice of card, and ask him for the position of the chosen card. Let us assume that the chosen card was eleventh from the top of the pack. In this case, you would count down to the eleventh card and ask the spectator to confirm that it really is the card he memorized. As the spectator is turning over the eleventh card, you palm off the top (twelfth) card from the pack, using your right hand. When the spectator

81

discovers that the card at the eleventh position is not his, you ask him for the name of his card. You then exclaim 'How amazing! That is the very card I put in my pocket!' as you mime the action of putting a card in your pocket. What you are actually doing at this point is dropping the palmed card into your pocket. You immediately turn the palm of your right hand outward to push open the top of your pocket, and then invite the spectator to take the card from your pocket and to confirm that it really is his card.

Tips

As with many other tricks, timing is critical here. You must avoid any hasty movements, or the audience will catch you out. Try to keep all attention focused on the spectator, by talking and joking with him, as this will help to conceal what you are really doing.

Position the Card

A card is selected from the pack by a spectator, shown to the audience, and then returned to the pack. Another spectator is then asked to choose any number and the card selected by the first spectator is found at that position in the pack.

Type	Location
Skill level	Moderate
Special techniques	Break control, double lift, riffle shuffle
Equipment	Pack of cards

Performance

Ask a spectator to take a card, show it to the audience and then return it to the pack. Lift up part of the pack so that the card can be placed on top of the lower portion of it, but use the break control (see pxxii) to bring the spectator's card to the top of the pack.

Next, give the cards a riffle shuffle (see pxi) but allow one card to fall on top of the spectator's card at the end of the shuffle. Turn over the top card and ask the spectator if this is his card. Naturally he will say 'No' and you then place the card back on top of the pack, face up, as you say 'Oh, that's good, because sometimes the card will come to the top of the pack of its own accord.' As you are talking, prepare for a double lift (see pxx) and turn to a second spectator, asking him to choose any number between 10 and 20.

Lift off the top two cards using the double lift (of course, the audience think there is only one card) and, saying 'one', move these cards about 2cm toward the rear of the pack (see illustration opposite).

Now, counting each card, pull one card at a time from the top of the pack, turning each one, face up, on top of the card (actually, two cards) first drawn until you reach the selected number.

Push the face-up cards flush with the rest of the pack and then fan them off into your right hand as you turn to the first spectator with the question 'Is your card among these?' Naturally he will say 'No'. Ask him to take the next (face-down) card, apparently the card at the number chosen, and turn it over – it is his card!

Psychic Spectator

A card is chosen by a spectator, and is then shuffled back into half of the pack. The chosen card is then named by a second spectator.

Type	Mind-reading
Skill level	Easy
Special techniques	None
Equipment	Pack of cards

Preparation
Separate the red cards from the black cards and then reassemble the pack, with the red cards forming the top half and the black cards making up the bottom half.

Performance
Divide the pack into two exact halves and place them side by side on the table. Now ask a spectator to take any card from one half of the pack, to remember it, and then to place it anywhere in the other half of the pack. Pick up the half-pack containing the spectator's card and give it a good shuffle before approaching a second spectator. Spread the cards out, so that the second spectator can see all

the faces and say 'I want you to make your mind as receptive as possible, pick out any card that stands out from the others, and then place it, face down, on the table.' If you have chosen the second spectator carefully, he will go along with your request and pick out the only card that is of a different colour to the rest.

Ask the first spectator to name his card and then turn over the card on the table, as you ask the audience to give a round of applause to the second spectator for his fantastic psychic ability. While the applause is ringing out, casually pick up all the cards and give them a quick shuffle to remove all traces of the special arrangement of the cards.

Push Through

A card is shown to the audience by the performer. This is then pushed through the pack and is instantly transformed into a card that was chosen earlier.

Type	Transformation
Skill level	Moderate
Special techniques	False shuffle or false cut; double lift
Equipment	Pack of cards

Performance

Fan out the pack of cards and ask a spectator to take any card, look at it, show it to the rest of the audience and then return it to the top of the pack. Secretly use a false shuffle (see pxii) or a false cut (see pxvii) to keep the card on the top of the pack.

Use the double lift (see pxx), show the card (actually, the second card in the pack) to the audience and ask the spectator if this is his card. The spectator will, of course, say 'No.' Holding the two cards in your right hand, bring your right hand over the pack for an instant and secretly drop the second card back on top of the pack. Then, in one continuous movement, push the card you still hold into, straight through and out of the other side of the pack. Show this card to the audience, who will be amazed to see that it has now changed into the card chosen by the spectator.

Quick Reverse

The pack is shuffled and a spectator is asked to take a card, show it to the audience, and then to replace it in the pack. The cards are then shuffled by the performer, so that the spectator's card is completely lost in the pack. The top and bottom cards of the pack are shown, but neither is the chosen card. The pack is then cut and the cards are spread, face up, on the table. In the middle of the face-up spread, one face-down card can be seen. This is taken by the spectator, and it is revealed to be the card chosen earlier.

Type	Location
Skill level	Moderate
Special techniques	Break control, double lift, ribbon spread, complete cut
Equipment	Pack of cards

Performance

Ask a spectator to shuffle the pack and then to hand it back to you. Spread out the cards, face down, and ask another spectator to take any card, look at it, and to show it to the audience. Then close up the fan of cards, cut off about half of the cards, and ask the spectator to put his card on top of the bottom portion. Secretly bring the chosen card to the top of the pack using the break control (see pxxii).

Now appear to show the top card of the pack, as you say 'Is this your card?' However, what you actually do is perform a double lift (see pxx) which shows the second card from the top. Leave these two cards, face up, on the top of the pack and turn the pack over to show the bottom card, as you ask 'Is this your card?' The spectator will, of course, say 'No.' Now say 'So, your card is not at the bottom and it is not at the top.' As you are talking, use the fingers of your right hand to pull out the card at the bottom of the pack, turn it over, and then replace it on the bottom of the pack.

Next, give the pack a complete cut (see pxv) and then ribbon spread (see pxix) the cards, face up, on the table. The audience will see that there is one card that is face down in the face-up spread. Ask the spectator to name the card he chose, and then take out the face-down card. It is his card!

Remote Control

A card is chosen by a spectator and is returned to the pack. The cards are then cut several times, face down, and then a few times, face up. The audience are told that the chosen card is exactly halfway through the pack but that this is 'far too many cards to count' for the performer. Therefore the performer's magical powers are employed, causing the chosen card to rise up through the pack until it is at a more convenient position, which is then announced by the performer. The chosen card is found at the position stated by the performer. Amazingly, at no time are the cards touched by the performer.

Type	Location
Skill level	Moderate
Special techniques	Complete cut
Equipment	Pack of cards

Preparation
Put the cards from A♥ to 10♥, in numerical order, on the bottom of the pack, the Ace being the bottom card. Put two more cards beneath the Ace, so the order from the bottom of the pack is: any two cards, A♥, 2♥, 3♥, 4♥, 5♥, 6♥, 7♥, 8♥, 9♥, 10♥. Put the pack in its box.

Performance
Take the pack from its box and place it on the table as you ask a spectator to cut off about half of the pack. Ask him to shuffle the cards he holds and then to look at the top card and show it to the audience, before putting the cards he holds back on top of the pack. Then tell him to cut the cards, complete the cut (see pxv) and to do this a couple more times, 'to lose the card in the pack'. Now ask him to turn the pack face up, and to cut the cards (again completing the cut) several times until you ask him to stop. In fact what you do is wait until one of your set-up cards comes to view, and then ask the spectator to turn the pack, face down, on the table.

The card from your set-up, plus the two extra cards you added, tells you the position of the chosen card from the top of the pack. All you have to do is add two to the value of the heart card that is now at the bottom of the pack and the chosen card will be dealt out at that number. So, if the spectator cuts the pack to 5♥, that number plus the two cards gives seven. Therefore the chosen card will be the seventh from the top of the pack when the pack is turned face down. Then say 'Your card is exactly halfway down the pack, but that is far too many cards to count, so please put your finger on top of the pack.' As soon as the spectator puts his finger on the pack, call out 'Stop!' Then say 'Your card is now 19th from the top of the pack, but that's still far too many to count, so please put your finger on the pack again. Stop! Your card is now 14th from the top of the pack, but that's still too many to count, so please put your finger on the pack again. Stop! Your card is now seventh (taking the example above) from the top of the pack. Please count off seven cards.' Ask him for the name of his chosen card, and it will be revealed when he turns over the seventh card. Prepare to take your applause!

Royal Families

The performer's amazing affinity with the cards is demonstrated by his ability to separate the Kings from the Queens, and then to pair them in suits, the cards being held all the while behind his back.

Type	Skill demonstration
Skill level	Easy
Special techniques	None
Equipment	Pack of cards

Performance

Ask a spectator to go through the pack and pick out all the Kings and all the Queens. You then pick up the cards in pairs, with a King and Queen as each pair, so the order is K, Q, K, Q, K, Q, K, Q (the suits of each pair do not have to match).

Ask another spectator to cut (but not shuffle) this packet of eight cards several times. Then take the packet behind your back and quickly take the first, third, fifth and seventh card into your right hand, leaving the other four in your left hand.

Next bring both hands forward and throw the cards, face up, onto the table. Thanks to your amazing dexterity, you have separated the Kings and Queens into two separate lots.

Now pick up the Queens and place the Kings on top of them. Do this casually, but ensure that the suits of the Kings are in the same order as those of the Queens. Again, ask a spectator to cut the packet of cards several times 'to mix them up', and then take the packet behind your back once again. As soon as the cards are out of sight of the audience, simply cut the cards in the middle, into two sets of four cards. Take the top card from each set and place the pair, face down, on the table. Then do the same with the remaining cards. Turn over the pairs and it will be seen that each King is paired with the Queen of the same suit.

Sandwich Surprise

The two red Aces are placed, face down, on the table. Any card is taken from the pack by a spectator, and this is then put, face up, between the two Aces. The red Aces are then moved apart and it is seen that the spectator's card has disappeared. It is discovered later, sandwiched face down between the two black Aces, which are themselves face up, in the middle of the pack.

Type	Transposition
Skill level	Advanced
Special techniques	Double lift, ribbon spread
Equipment	Pack of cards

Preparation

Put A♠, face up, on the bottom of the face-down pack. Put the two red Aces, with A♣ between them, face down, on the top of the pack, so that the top three cards are A♦, A♣ and A♥.

Performance

Hold the pack in your left hand and, with your right hand, lift off the top card (A♦), and show it to the audience. Put the card back on top of the pack and immediately deal it off, face down, onto the table, as you say 'Ace of Diamonds'. You now appear to do exactly the same with the next card, but you really perform a double lift (see pxx), to show A♥. Again, put the card (in fact, two cards) back on top of the pack and immediately deal the top (single) card, face down, onto the table, next to the first one, as you say 'Ace of Hearts'. The audience will believe that there are two red Aces on the table, but in fact the two cards are A♦ and A♣.

Now spread the pack of cards, face down, between your hands and ask a spectator to take any card (be careful not to expose the face-up A♠ on the bottom of the pack). Then ask the spectator to turn his card face up and to slide it between the two cards on the table (see illustration 1 below).

As he is doing this, lift up the top card of the pack a little and slip the little finger of your left hand beneath it.

Now pick up the three cards from the table and place them on top of the pack. Lift off the top four cards (the break caused by your little finger makes this easy) and turn them over on top of the pack. The audience will see the face-up A♥, as expected. Deal A♥, face up, onto the table, followed by the next card (A♦), and it seems that the spectator's card has disappeared. (It is actually the top card of the pack with A♣, face up, beneath it, but you must be careful not to reveal this.)

Next cut the top half of the pack to the bottom, and then ribbon spread (see pxix) the cards, face down, on the table. Much to everyone's surprise, the two black Aces are face up in the spread, with one face-down card sandwiched between them (see illustration 2 below).

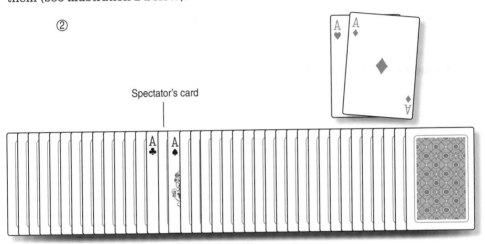

② Spectator's card

Ask the spectator to take the face-down card and to show the audience that it is the one he chose earlier.

Tips

When you lift off A♦ at the start of this trick, do it as if you were performing a double lift (although, in this case, you are lifting only one card). This will mean that when you carry out the next move (when you are indeed performing a double lift), there will be no telltale difference in your movements.

Second Sight

A pack of cards is shuffled and the performer's fantastic mental powers are used to name the top few cards before they are dealt.

Type	Mind-reading
Skill level	Advanced
Special techniques	Glimpse
Equipment	Pack of cards

Performance

Ask a spectator to shuffle the pack and then return it to you. As you take the pack from him, get a glimpse (see pxxiii) of the top card. This is not too difficult to do undetected as no one knows what you are about to do and, as you are telling the audience all about your amazing mental powers, all attention will be on you and not on your hands. Alternatively, quickly get sight of the bottom card and then shuffle it to the top (see pxii).

Hold the pack in your left hand, with your thumb on one side, the ball of the thumb resting against the top card. Your forefinger should be at the end of the pack, with its tip touching the top card, and your other three fingers should be along the right side of the pack.

You then name the top (glimpsed) card and apparently lift it off the pack, and throw it, face up, on the table. What you actually do, though, is lift the end nearest you with your right thumb and lift the end of the second card as well, rather like preparing for a double lift (see pxx). You then lift the two cards at the rear just high enough for you to see the index of the second card. Allow the second card to drop back onto the pack as you take the top card, and throw it onto the table.

You will find that, as the second card falls, it is stopped by the heel of your thumb, which causes a slight break (see illustration below).

This makes it much easier to lift the next two cards (as if they were a single card) as you name the new top card. Take the top card and throw it, face up, on the table as the second card is allowed to fall back onto the heel of your thumb as before.

Repeat the process to name a few more cards, but do not do too many or someone may work out what you are up to.

Seeing Things

A card is chosen by a spectator and is put, sight unseen, into his pocket. Another spectator is also asked to choose a card. The pack is then examined by the performer, but the card chosen by the second spectator has vanished. The first spectator is then asked to take the card from his pocket, and it is shown to be the same card chosen by the second person!

Type	Transposition
Skill level	Advanced
Special techniques	Force, palm
Equipment	Pack of cards, a special card

Preparation
Make a special card (see On the Move p71). If you have already made a special card for On the Move, be sure to use different cards this time. Put this special card at the bottom of the pack and the duplicate of the rear card of the special card on top of the pack. Make sure that the glued end of the special card is at the end of the pack that will be closer to your body when performing the trick (see illustration below).

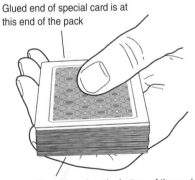

Glued end of special card is at this end of the pack

Special card on the bottom of the pack

Performance

Ask a spectator to take a card, but actually force (see pxiii) the top card. Tell the spectator to put the card in his pocket, without looking at it. Meanwhile, cut the pack in order to bring the special card into the middle of the pack.

Riffle the ends of the cards as you ask a second spectator to call out 'Stop!' at any time. As the special card is near the middle of the pack you can, with practice, always stop at this card, no matter when the spectator calls 'Stop!' Open up the pack a little and ask the spectator to look at, and remember, the card that you stopped at (this will be the rear card of the special card, the duplicate of which is in the first spectator's pocket).

Ask the second spectator to call out the name of his card and then deal the cards, face up, onto the table. The chosen card has apparently vanished because the special card will go down onto the table as one card, with the value of the front card now showing.

All you now have to do is to ask the first spectator to take out his card and show the audience that it is the very same card that the second spectator saw in the pack just moments before. As this is being done, you have ample opportunity to palm (see pxxii) the special card secretly from the pack and put it in your pocket.

Shazam!

The pack is dealt into two piles by a spectator and one of these is then chosen by him. The bottom card of this pile is revealed to the audience before the pack is reassembled. The spectator is then asked to deal the cards into four piles. Once again, the pack is reassembled, and the magic word 'Shazam!' is spelled out, with one card being moved for each letter of the word. When the next card is turned over, it is seen to be the card shown to the audience earlier.

Type	Location
Skill level	Easy
Special techniques	None
Equipment	Pack of cards

Performance

Ask a spectator to deal the pack into two piles, to pick either one of them and show the bottom card to the audience, and then to put the card back on top of the other pile. You then place the pile topped by the chosen card underneath the other pile, and ask the spectator to deal the pack from left to right, into four piles.

Pick up the piles of cards and reassemble the pack, making sure that the second pile dealt by the spectator is now the top portion of the pack. As you hand the whole pack to the spectator, say to him 'I think that you will agree that the card shown to the audience is now well and truly lost in the pack, so we will have to use a magic word to find it.' Tell him that the magic word is 'Shazam!' and ask him to spell that word, dealing one card from the top of the pack for each letter. Ask the audience for the name of the card they saw earlier and, when they reply, invite the spectator to turn over the next card. It is the chosen card!

Sim Sala Bim

A spectator is asked to memorize one of several cards that have been shown to him, and the cards are then mixed up thoroughly. Although the identity of the chosen card is only in the spectator's mind, it is revealed by the performer after intoning the magic words 'Sim Sala Bim'.

Type	Location
Skill level	Easy
Special techniques	None
Equipment	Pack of cards

Performance

Shuffle the pack and deal out, face up, three rows of seven overlapping cards. For a typical arrangement, see the illustration below.

Ask a spectator to memorize any one of the cards on the table and then to tell you which row it is in. Gather up the cards in each row into a pile and put the pile containing the chosen card between the other two piles.

Turn the cards over and deal the cards out into three piles. Show each pile in turn to the spectator and ask him which pile contains his card. Again, put this pile between the other two and deal the cards out into three piles. Show each pile to the spectator and again ask which pile holds his memorized card. Once again, place the chosen pile between the other two piles. Then take the collected cards, turn them face down, and invoke the magic spell 'Sim Sala Bim', moving one card from the top to the bottom of the packet for each letter. Ask the spectator for the name of his chosen card and then turn over the next card – it is the very same card!

Tips

'Sim Sala Bim' were the magic words used by a great magician called Dante, so you could do some research on him and weave the trick around the story of this master of magic.

This trick, which is at least two hundred years old, will work with any word or words of ten letters. The author uses his own name to spell out the cards and you can do the same if your name, or that of one of your spectators, contains ten letters. You could use phrases or names, such as 'That's Magic' (you will have to ignore the apostrophe), 'Hocus Pocus', 'Magic Spell', 'Mumbo Jumbo', 'Will It Work?', or even 'Fred Bloggs'.

Sorted

Six cards are shown to be well mixed, with alternating colours. However, having been counted by the performer, they have been sorted by colour and into numerical order.

Type	Transposition
Skill level	Advanced
Special techniques	Glide
Equipment	Pack of cards

Performance

Sort through the cards, take out A♠, 2♠, 3♠ and 4♥, 5♥, 6♥, and arrange them in the following order from face to back: A♠, 5♥, 3♠, 4♥, 2♠, 6♥ (see illustration 1 opposite).

Show these cards to the audience and point out that the colours alternate black and red but that they are not in numerical order.

Square up the packet of six cards and hold it, face down, in your left hand. Turn your hand over, to show A♠ on the bottom of the packet and then turn your hand back down again. With your right hand, pull out the bottom card (A♠) and place it, face down, on top of the packet as you say 'black'. Then draw out the next card from the bottom and show it, face up, before placing it on top of the packet as you say 'red'.

Next turn the packet over, to show 3♠, and say 'black'. As you turn the packet back over again, appear to take the bottom card in your right hand and place it, face down, on top of the packet. In fact, you perform the glide (see pxx) so that it is really the card second from the bottom that you take.

Still holding the packet of cards face down, draw out the bottom card, say 'red', placing it, face down, on top of the packet. Draw out the next card from the bottom, and turn it over, to show 2♠. Place this card, face down, on top of the packet. Turn up the packet in your left hand, so that the audience can see the bottom card (6♥), and then turn it face down again, as you perform the glide and put the card on top of the packet. Again, although you apparently take the card from the bottom of the packet, you actually take the second-bottom card.

It appears that you have taken the cards, one at a time, from the bottom to the top of the packet, without any false moves. However, when you turn the cards over and fan them out, the reds and blacks have, amazingly, separated themselves and are now in the correct numerical order (see illustration 2).

Tips
It is important that you do not show anyone this trick until you can perform the glide effortlessly and at the same speed with which you are able to draw out a single card from the bottom and place it on the top of the packet. Every move, both genuine and fake, should look exactly the same, in order for the trick to be convincing.

Speedy Change

Two cards are shown to the audience, one of which is held behind the performer's back. This card is immediately transformed into the other card that was shown.

Type	Transposition
Skill level	Moderate
Special techniques	None
Equipment	Two special cards

Preparation
Make two special cards. Take any two cards from a spare pack and glue them face to face, making sure that the glue extends right to the edges of the two cards (you can wipe off any excess afterwards). Then take two more cards and glue them back to back (we will assume that these two cards are 5♣ and Q♥). Magicians call two cards glued face to face to make one card a 'double backer' because there is a back design on each side; the other card described here is known as a 'double facer' because there is a face card on each side.

Performance
Hold the two cards between the thumb and first two fingers of your right hand (with the thumb underneath and the fingers on top), with the double backer on top of the double facer showing Q♥ (see illustration 1 below).

①
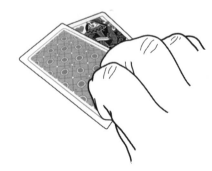

Now turn your hand over, at the same time moving your thumb to the right, thus changing the position of the two cards, so that the other card (5♣) is seen (see illustration 2 below).

②

Take 5♣ in your left hand, and say '5♣'. Then hold it behind your back for a second, turn it over and bring it forward again, to show that it has changed to Q♥, as you say 'Q♥, for 5♣ is ... here'. As you say this, place the double facer with Q♥ on top of the double backer, with your thumb underneath and the fingers on top, then turn the two cards over, moving your thumb to the right as you do so, to show 5♣.

Tips

Although the double cards described here will be adequate for this trick, purpose-made cards with the thickness of a single card can be obtained from magic shops and are much easier to handle.

If you look at the relative position of the two cards in the illustrations, you will see that all is not as it should be in illustration 2 above. If you were using ordinary cards, 5♣ would be underneath the face-down card but, provided that you keep the trick moving at an even pace (without racing through it), the audience will not notice this.

Spell It

A number of cards are removed from the pack by a spectator, and one of these is chosen by him. All of the cards are returned to the pack and then the name of the chosen card is spelled out by the spectator himself, moving one card for each letter. The next card after the final letter is revealed to be his card.

Type	Location
Skill level	Easy
Special techniques	None
Equipment	Pack of cards

Preparation
Take from the pack the four, five, nine, Jack and King of both Spades and Hearts and the three, seven, eight and Queen of Clubs. Mix them up and then put these 14 cards on top of the pack and place four more cards on top of them. You must memorize the name of the fifth card (ie the first of your 14 specially-selected cards).

Performance
Ask a spectator to deal off, from the top of the pack, between five and ten cards onto the table, while you turn your back to the audience. Suggest that he does this as quietly as possible so that you cannot hear how many cards he deals.

Now ask the spectator to deal the same number of cards into a second pile. You then tell him to look at and remember the card at the bottom of the second pile, and then to put that pile back on top of the pack, leaving the first pile on the table. When he has done this, turn back to face the audience and say 'It is impossible for me to know how many cards you dealt, or the identity of the card you have chosen, so I am going to ask you to find it yourself. All you have to do is spell out the name of your card, taking one card from the pack for each letter and then turn over the next card.' To illustrate what you would like the spectator to do, you deal off one card for each letter of the card you have memorized, pretending that this is a random card and then turn over the next card. This will not be the card you have spelled for this demonstration, but it is really a crafty way of reversing the order of the top twelve cards, for all the cards set up have twelve letters. Place the turned-over card back, face down, on top of the pack and put the dealt cards back on the pack as well.

Then, pretend that you have just realized that the first of the spectator's two piles of cards is still on the table. Ask him to put these cards back on the top of the pack and then to spell out the name of his card, dealing one card for each letter. The next card will be the card he selected.

Tips

To save you from having to remember a different card each time, always put the same card in the fifth position before you start.

The spelling must include the word 'of' (eg 'K-I-N-G-O-F-S-P-A-D-E-S').

If you prefer, you can give a false shuffle (see pxii) before you start the trick, retaining the top 18 cards on top.

Spellbound

The card chosen by a spectator is found by counting out other cards from the pack to spell its name – but there are a couple of other surprises along the way.

Type	Location
Skill level	Moderate
Special techniques	False shuffle
Equipment	Pack of cards

Preparation

Arrange the following cards on top of the pack, reading from the top down: A♣, 2♠, 6♠, 9♦, 3♣, 10♣, 3♥, 8♠, A♠, 5♣, 2♣, 6♦, any ♥, 10♠, any 3, any 9, any card, any 3 and any 8.

Performance

Give the cards a false shuffle (see pxii), retaining the 19-card set-up at the top. Then push eight cards from the top of the pack, show them to a spectator and ask him to take one card without letting you see it. Put the cards that were below the one chosen back on top of the pack, and place the cards that were above the chosen card on the bottom of the pack. Then give the pack another false shuffle, keeping the top portion of the pack at the top.

Next, ask the spectator to deal off cards from the top of the pack, one for each letter of the suit of the chosen card (eg D-I-A-M-O-N-D-S). When the card representing the last letter of the suit of his chosen card is turned over, it is one of the very same suit. Now ask the spectator to spell out the value of the card, again dealing one card for each letter of the word (eg N-I-N-E). The card that the spectator turns over when saying the last letter of the value of his chosen card is, magically, also of the same value as the chosen card.

Straw Poll

A card is selected and then returned to the pack by a spectator. Then it is magically identified by a psychic drinking straw!

Type	Location
Skill level	Easy
Special techniques	Glimpse
Equipment	Pack of cards, drinking straw

Performance

Show the drinking straw to the audience and tell them, with all seriousness, that it has amazing psychic abilities. Place the straw on the table in front of you and ask a spectator to shuffle the pack. Then ask another spectator to take a card from the pack and show it to the audience. As this is being done, get a glimpse (see pxxiii) of the bottom card of the pack.

Ask the spectator to place his card on top of the pack, and then cut the pack, taking the top half to the bottom, to bring the chosen card to the centre. Cut the pack a few more times to make sure that no one knows the location of the chosen card.

Turn the pack face up and pass the cards, one at a time, over the psychic straw. When you reach the chosen card, the straw moves! It does so because you blow gently when the chosen card comes into view. You know which card is the chosen card because it will be the one to the right of the card you glimpsed at the bottom of the pack earlier (see illustration below).

Spectator's card

Original bottom card

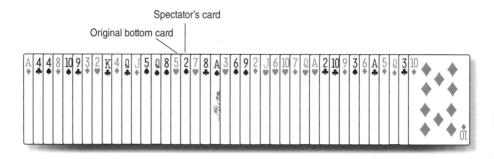

Sure-Fire Bet

The audience are misled into thinking that the performer has lost the bet that he made with them: he announces that the next card turned over will be the card chosen by a spectator, even though that card has been dealt already. However, the performer wins the bet for the next card turned over is indeed the card chosen by the spectator.

Type	Location
Skill level	Easy
Special techniques	Glimpse
Equipment	Pack of cards

Performance

Ask a spectator to shuffle the pack and, when you take it back from him, glimpse (see pxxiii) the bottom card. Spread out the cards, face down, between your hands and ask the spectator to choose one of them. Cut the pack at the point where the selection was made and place the top portion of the pack on the table. Ask the spectator to show his card to the rest of the audience and then to place it on top of the cards on the table. Drop the rest of the cards you are holding on top of the chosen card 'so that it is lost back in its original position'. (This is not true but the audience will not realize this.) Pick up the pack and give it a few cuts 'to lose the chosen card'. (This is another lie because the cuts will not separate the chosen card and the 'key card' – the card that you saw earlier at the bottom of the pack.)

Start dealing the cards, face up, onto the table, and say 'We are now going to have a little bet.' Keep dealing until you have gone several cards past the chosen card (which will be the first one after your key card) and, as you begin to draw off another card, say 'I bet you that the next card I turn over will be your card'. As the spectator has already seen his card dealt, he is confident that the card you are about to turn over is not his card and he will take up the challenge. You now pick up the chosen card from the table (the one next to your key card) and turn it face down on the table – you have won the bet!

Tips

To make the trick even more entertaining, you could invite the spectator to bet some of his own money or, say, his watch. You can generously return this to him when he loses the bet!

Swap

The position of two cards is changed by magic.

Type	Transposition
Skill level	Moderate
Special techniques	Double lift
Equipment	Pack of cards

Performance

Shuffle the pack and apparently turn over the top card, face up, onto the pack. However, what you are actually doing is a double lift (see pxx) so that it is really the second card that the audience see. Let us assume that this is 6♦. Turn the card (in fact, two cards) face down again on top of the pack, then lift only the top card and place it on the table, as you say 'six of Diamonds' (or whatever the card was).

Now do another double lift to show the next card at the top of the pack. Again it is the second card that the audience see. (Let us assume that this is 8♠.) As before, turn these two cards back, face down, on the top of the pack. Next, place the (actual) top card face down on the table as you say 'eight of Spades'. You then reinforce what you have just done by pointing to the first card and reminding everyone that it is 6♦. Pick up this card, place it face down on top of the pack and then do a double lift to show that it has changed to 8♠. Then turn over the card on the table (the one the audience believe to be 8♠) and everyone will see that it is now 6♦ – the two cards have changed places by magic.

Telephone Trickery

A card, chosen by a spectator, is shown to the audience, but not to the performer. The spectator is then asked to make a telephone call to a friend of the performer, who correctly identifies the spectator's card.

Type	Mind-reading
Skill level	Advanced
Special techniques	Force
Equipment	Pack of cards, two copies of a table of codes

Preparation

Write out two copies of the table of codes below. Give one copy to the friend who is to be telephoned, and keep the other copy yourself.

Monday	8♣, K♥, 3♠
Tuesday	10♦, 2♣, 7♥
Wednesday	9♠, 5♦, Q♣
Thursday	4♥, A♠, 6♦
Friday	J♣, 8♥, K♠
Saturday	3♦, 10♣, 2♥
Sunday	7♠, 9♦, 5♣

There are three cards listed against each day of the week, in case you want to perform the trick more than once, or there are some people in your audience who may have seen you perform the trick previously.

Look closely at the table and you will see that the cards are in the same order as the Eight Kings sequence (see pxix). This is not absolutely necessary, but it does make the cards easier to remember. (It is a good idea to keep the table handy, though, just in case you forget the sequence!)

Performance

During your performance of a previous trick, get the appropriate card (according to the table) to the top of the pack. So, for example, if the performance is taking place for the second time on a Tuesday, you would use 2♣. You now have to force (see pxiii) that card on a spectator and then hand him the telephone and ask him to ring your friend, who will tell him which card he has taken.

When your friend answers the telephone, he has simply to look at his copy of the chart to know which card has been taken. So, for example, if it was the third call made to him on Friday, it would be K♠.

103

Tips
You should not perform this trick if you have performed Make a Call (see p60) for the same audience: although the methods are completely different, the tricks are too similar in type and the audience might find this tedious.

Think a Spell

A few cards are taken at random from the pack by the performer, and a spectator is asked to think of one of them before returning the cards to the pack. The pack is shuffled and the spectator is asked for the name of his chosen card. Its name is then spelled out, one card being dealt for each letter. When the card representing the final letter of the name is turned over, it is seen to be the spectator's card.

Type	Location
Skill level	Moderate
Special techniques	Stacked pack, false shuffle
Equipment	Pack of cards

Preparation
Stack the cards in the Eight Kings sequence (see pxix).

Performance
After performing a couple of tricks which use the Eight Kings sequence, casually cut the pack so that 6♣ is on the face and J♥ is the top card. Run through the face-down pack and throw the seventh, eleventh, 17th, 22nd, 38th and 44th cards, face down, on the table. Try not to make it obvious that you are counting the cards as you do this, and appear to be simply throwing out the cards at random. Thanks to the secret arrangement of the pack, the cards you throw out will be 7♦, 4♦, 3♥, 5♠, A♠ and 10♣. Pick up the six cards and spread them out, so that the spectator can see the faces, and ask him to concentrate on one of them. Be careful not to change the position of any of the cards as you do this.

Then take the pack, push the top nine cards to one side and insert the group of six cards (in their original order), face down, at that point. Next give the cards a false shuffle (see pxii), keeping these 15 cards at the top of the pack.

Now all you have to do is ask for the name of the chosen card, and spell down to it, dealing one card, face down, for each letter. When you come to the card representing the final letter, turn it over and it will be the very card that the spectator is thinking of.

Tips
If you do several tricks using the Eight Kings sequence, this will have to be the last one that you perform as it destroys the sequence of the cards.

This Isn't Your Card

A card is chosen by a spectator, shown to the audience, and returned to the pack. The cards are then shuffled by the performer, 'so that the card is lost'. Another spectator is then asked to cut the pack into three portions. The bottom card of each portion is shown to the audience and is then placed, face down, on the table, as the performer states that each one is not the chosen card (although one of them is indeed the chosen card). A card is then taken from the pack and is held, face down, by the performer, who announces that this is the chosen card. The audience think that the performer has made a mistake for they believe that the chosen card is one of those already placed on the table. However, the performer has the last laugh when the card is turned over and it is indeed the chosen card!

Type	Location
Skill level	Moderate
Special techniques	Break control, false shuffle, glide
Equipment	Pack of cards

Performance
Ask a spectator to shuffle the pack and then to hand it back to you. Spread the cards, face down, between your hands and ask a second spectator to take any card, show it to the audience, and then to return it to the pack. Secretly bring the chosen card to the top of the pack, using the break control (see pxxii). Next give the cards a false shuffle (see pxii), to move the chosen card from the top to the bottom of the pack, and then place the pack, face down, on the table.

Ask a third spectator to lift off about two-thirds of the cards and to place them to the right of the remaining cards. Then tell him to cut off about half of the larger portion of cards and to place this portion to the right of the first two portions. You then pick up the last portion cut and show the bottom card to the audience. Turn the cards face down and draw out the bottom card, which you place, face down, on the table. As you do this, say to the second spectator 'This is not your card.' Do exactly the same with the middle portion and then pick up the third portion (which was originally the bottom part of the pack). Show the bottom card and again say 'This is not your card.' This is, of course, his card and some people in the audience may laugh or point out your 'mistake'. However, just ignore them and appear to draw out the bottom card and place it on the table with the other

105

two. What you really do is perform the glide (see pxx) so that it is the card immediately above the bottom card which goes down on the table.

Draw out the next card (the card above the chosen card) and use it as a pointer to point to the three cards, as you say 'None of these is your chosen card.' Again, this may cause some reaction from the audience, but you simply ignore this. Put the pointer card back on the bottom of the pack, as you ask a fourth spectator to call out any number, from three to twelve. Say to the second spectator 'I will now find your card at that number from the bottom of the pack.' Let us assume that the number called out is seven. In this case, you would pull the first card from the bottom of the pack, turn it face up, and place it on the table. Then you would perform the glide, so that you do not draw out the bottom card, but rather the five cards above it, which you would then place, one by one, face up, on the table. For the seventh card, you really pull out the bottom (chosen) card and hold it, face down, in your hand as you boldly state that it is the chosen card. Ask the second spectator for the name of his card and then look rather apprehensive, as if you have just realized that you have made a mistake. At this point someone may call out that the chosen card is on the table. You can allow them to turn this card over to show that they are mistaken before you reveal, to the audience's complete amazement, that the card you hold really is the chosen card. If no one challenges you, you should simply look at the card in your hand, without showing it to the audience, and say 'I am right. This is the chosen card.' At this point someone is bound to call your bluff, whereupon you turn over the card you are holding to show that it really is the chosen card!

Thought Transfer

The cards that several spectators will choose are predicted by the performer's psychic assistant.

Type	Mind-reading
Skill level	Moderate
Special techniques	Force, stacked pack
Equipment	Pack of cards, notepad (without covers), felt pen, cardboard box

Preparation

Stack the pack in the Eight Kings sequence (see pxix). You will also need to know the name of a member of your audience. Write this person's initials (say, JP) in large letters, on one side of the notepad.

Performance

Your assistant sits facing the audience with the notepad on her lap, the page with the initials on it face down.

You approach a spectator and ask for the initials of his name. Let us say that these are JF. Your assistant then writes 'JF' on the clean sheet on top of the notepad, and holds it up for everyone to see. You now tell the audience that your assistant is going to write a message on the pad. She places the pad on her lap, turning it over as she does so, and writes 'nine of Diamonds' on the sheet that bears the initials 'JP', then folds the sheet and drops it into the box.

You then ask JF to take a card from the pack. Let us assume that he takes 4♣. Next, you cut the cards at the place from which the card was taken and, as you move towards a second spectator, hold the pack in such a way that your assistant can see the bottom card (in this case, Q♦). As she understands the Eight Kings sequence, she can work out which card was taken by the first spectator.

You then ask the second spectator for his initials (say, DH), and your assistant writes them on the pad and holds this up for the audience to see. As she puts the pad back down on her lap, she turns it over so the initials of the first person (JF) are facing her. Alongside the initials of JF, she writes 'four of Clubs', then folds the paper and drops it into the box. You now ask DH to take a card. Once again, you cut the pack at the point from which the card was taken, so that your assistant can see the bottom card. If we assume that the bottom card is 6♠, your assistant then knows that DH has got J♦.

Now you approach the spectator whose name you know (JP) and, when he gives his name, your assistant writes 'JP' on the pad and holds it up to show the audience. She then turns the pad and writes 'Jack of Diamonds' against the initials of DH. While she is doing this, you take the opportunity to look through the pack to find 9♦, which you then force (see pxiii) on JP.

Next you ask another spectator to pick up the box, take out one of the folded sheets of paper, and call out the initials on it. The spectator whose initials these are is then asked which card he took, and the person holding the sheet of paper confirms that the same card was predicted by your assistant. You follow the same procedure with the other two sheets of paper and, astoundingly, all three predictions are correct!

Tips

There is a danger that someone may actually take 9♦, or whatever card you and your assistant have previously arranged to force. To avoid this happening, put a small pencil mark, at the top left-hand corner and bottom right-hand corner, on the back of this card. When the first two spectators are taking a card, keep an eye out for the pencil mark and make sure that it is not taken.

Totally Correct

While the performer's back is turned, a pack of cards is dealt into several random piles by a spectator. Having turned back to face the audience, the performer announces the total value of the cards at the bottom of the piles, even though none of the cards was seen by him.

Type	Mind-reading
Skill level	Moderate
Special techniques	None
Equipment	Pack of cards

Performance

Ask a spectator to shuffle the cards. Explain to him that you are going to turn your back to the audience and give him some instructions which he is to follow very carefully. With your back turned, tell him to look at the top card of the pack and then to place it, face down, on the table. Next ask him to deal cards, face down, on top of the card on the table to make the value up to twelve. So, if the first card is a five, he will add seven cards to it to make it up to twelve; if it is a nine, he will add only three cards.

Now ask him to look at the new top card of the pack, to place it, face down, on the table, near to the first pile, and again to add enough cards to make the value up to twelve, remembering that picture cards count as ten and Aces count as one for this trick. Ask him to continue like this all the way through the pack. If, when he gets towards the end of the pack, he does not have enough cards to make twelve, he is to put the remaining cards to one side. Ask him to let you know when he has finished, so that you can then turn back to face the audience.

When you are once again facing the audience, secretly count how many piles there are. Subtract four from that number and multiply the result by 13. If there are any discarded cards, add that number to your total. This will be the sum of all the values of the cards at the bottom of the piles, which you can then announce.

Turn the bottom card of each pile over and add together their values and, sure enough, you are right!

Here is an example of how this works. When you turn around, you see that there are eight piles on the table. Take four from this number, giving you four. Then multiply four by 13, which makes 52. Pick up the discarded cards (of which there are two) and add on this number, making 54. When you turn the piles over to show the bottom cards, these will also add up to 54 (see illustration opposite).

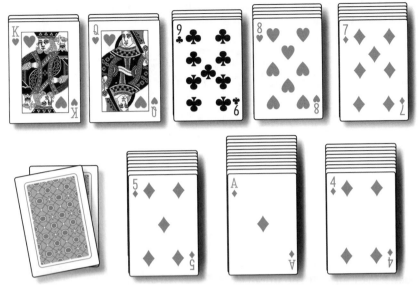

Tips

To make certain that the spectator understands your instructions, you can demonstrate what you would like him to do by dealing out a couple of piles. The spectator can then shuffle the cards again as you turn away from the audience.

Touch of Magic

A pack of cards is spread out, with the faces towards a spectator. The spectator is asked to touch just one card, then the spread of cards is closed up and the pack is shuffled. The pack is squared and suddenly the card touched by the spectator appears, face up, on top of the face-down pack.

Type	Location
Skill level	Advanced
Special techniques	Crimp, overhand shuffle
Equipment	Pack of cards

Performance

Ask a spectator to shuffle the cards and then to hand the pack back to you. Go to another spectator, spread the cards out between your hands, with the faces towards the spectator, and ask him to touch any card. Spread the cards wider where the spectator is touching the card and ask him to allow another spectator to see which card is being touched. As this is being done, use your left thumb, behind the cards, to push against and crimp (see pxxiii) the bottom left-hand corner of the card touched by the spectator (see illustration 1 below).

①

Then close up the cards and give them an overhand shuffle (see pxi), so that the chosen card is lost in the pack. As you hold the cards in your left hand, you will be able to see the crimp clearly at the end of the pack nearer you. Bring your right hand over and lift the upper part of the pack until you can insert your left thumb beneath the crimped (chosen) card. With the ball of your thumb against the face of the chosen card, move your thumb to the left, moving the chosen card to the left as well. Continue with this pushing movement to the left until the card is about a third of the way out of the pack (see illustration 2 below) and then push upwards and to the right so that the card moves around the side of the pack and ends up, face up, on top of the pack.

②

Just before the card has turned over, move your right hand away and the chosen card will appear, as if by magic, on top of the pack.

Tips

Practise this trick until you can get the chosen card to the top of the pack very quickly, as this will create the best effect.

Transmutation

The card on the face of the pack is transformed into another when the performer passes his hand over it.

Type	Transformation
Skill level	Advanced
Special techniques	None
Equipment	Pack of cards

Performance

Hold the pack of cards in your left hand, with the bottom card facing the audience. One of the long sides of the pack rests on the first joint of your middle, third and fourth fingers, and the other long side is held by your thumb; your left forefinger should be resting on one of the short ends of the pack.

Move your right hand until it covers the whole of the face card and then secretly use the nail of your left forefinger to push the bottom card towards you and into the crotch of your right thumb. Move your right hand (which now conceals the bottom card) very briefly to your right, giving the audience a glimpse of the face card. Immediately, move it back, once again covering the face card and giving you the opportunity to deposit the card from the bottom of the pack on the face of the pack. Bring your right hand to the right again, and the face card has changed to another.

Tips

This is not really a trick that can stand on its own when someone says 'Show me a trick!' However, it is a useful, quick item, to include in your performance with other tricks.

Transposition

The two black Kings are held by a spectator, while the performer has the two red Kings. Magically, ownership is reversed, with the black cards being transferred to the spectator, and the red cards to the performer.

Type	Transposition
Skill level	Moderate
Special techniques	Double lift
Equipment	Pack of cards

Performance

Go though the pack and remove the four Kings which you then hold, face down, in your left hand, with the two black cards in the middle and the red cards in the top and bottom positions (see illustration below).

As you close up the fan with your right hand, slip the little finger of your left hand beneath the second card. Now appear to lift off the top card, but actually perform a double lift (see pxx) and show the audience K♣. Put this card (actually, two cards) back on the packet of cards, and ask a spectator to hold out one hand. Take the (real) top card and place it, face down, on his palm. Ask him to put his other hand on top of the card, in order to prevent you tampering with it (in fact, the real reason is to stop him looking at the card).

Now count the cards from one hand to the other, as you say 'That leaves three cards.' (This actually reverses the order of the cards you hold.) Square up the packet of cards and again slip the tip of the little finger of your left hand under the second card from the top. Now do another double lift, to show K♠, which you apparently put on top of the first King held by the spectator. However, as before, it is the real top card that is dealt to the spectator. Again, ask the spectator to place his other hand on top of his cards, so that you 'cannot touch them'.

The audience now believe that the spectator has the two black Kings and that you have the two red Kings. Now wave your right hand mysteriously and ask the spectator to look at the cards he holds. Much to everyone's surprise, he has the two red Kings. You then turn over the two cards you hold, to show that the reds and blacks have magically changed places, for you now have the two black Kings.

Trapped

Trapped

The pack of cards is shuffled by a spectator, and the names of two cards are written on a piece of card by the performer. This piece of card is then initialled, on the reverse side, by a second spectator, to prove that it is not substituted at any point. The cards are spread across the table by the performer and a third spectator is asked to push the piece of card into the pack at any point. The cards are then gathered up and are spread between the performer's hands until the piece of card with the prediction is seen. The second spectator is then asked to confirm that his initials are indeed on the card and the cards are spread, face up, on the table. The card with the prediction and the cards on either side of it are then pushed forward out of the pack. The piece of card is picked up by the third spectator, to confirm that the performer has correctly predicted which two cards it was placed between.

Type	Mind-reading
Skill level	Advanced
Special techniques	Ribbon spread
Equipment	Pack of cards, pencil, small piece of card

Performance

Ask a spectator to shuffle the pack, then take it back and spread the cards, face up, between your hands, so that the audience can see that they are well mixed. In fact, what you are really doing is looking at the top and bottom cards of the pack. You must memorize these two cards and we will assume, for the purpose of illustration, that these are 7♣ and K♦. Close up the cards and place the pack, face down, on the table. Then pick up the piece of card and – without letting anyone see what you are writing – write on it the name of the top and bottom cards (in this case, 'the seven of Clubs and the King of Diamonds'). Then turn the piece of card over and ask a second spectator to write his initials on it.

Pick up the pack and ribbon spread (see pxix) it, face down, on the table. Ask a third spectator to insert the piece of card anywhere in the pack, and then to gather up all the cards. Remind the audience of what has happened so far, **113** saying 'This gentleman (the first spectator) shuffled the cards, this gentleman (the second spectator) initialled the piece of card and this gentleman (the third spectator) inserted it somewhere in the pack.' As you are talking, spread the cards, face down, between your hands until you come to the piece of card. Cut the pack at this point, taking the top half in your right hand and retaining the lower portion, with the piece of card on top of it, in your left hand, as you show the card to the second spectator and ask him to confirm his initials.

Then say 'I have written a prediction on this piece of card.' As you are talking, use your left thumb to push the piece of card onto the cards held in your right hand. If you lift the card slightly as you do so, the audience will see that you have written something on the card, but do not give them a chance to read the actual words. Place the cards from your left hand, face down, on top of the piece of card and the rest of the pack in your right hand. This sequence of moves will put the piece of card between the two cards you memorized earlier.

Ribbon spread the cards, face up, on the table and push out the piece of card and the playing card on either side of it. Say to the third spectator 'It seems that you put the piece of card between 7♣ and K♦. Will you please read my prediction.' To everyone's astonishment, your prediction is correct!

Tips
If you have a business card, you could use it for this trick and leave it with a spectator as a souvenir (and a useful reminder of your name).

Travelling Aces

Three Aces are magically transported from the pack, to join the fourth Ace in the card box.

Type	Transposition
Skill level	Advanced
Special techniques	None
Equipment	Pack of cards

Performance
Go through the pack and move the threes (except 3♠) and the four Aces to the bottom of the pack, as you say something like 'Let's try something with the four Aces.' The suits of the threes must be in the same order as the suits of the Aces and the A♠ must be the bottom card, so that the order at the bottom of the pack will be as shown in illustration 1 opposite. Note, however, that the cards must not be spread like this in performance as the audience must believe that you have simply brought four cards to the bottom of the pack.

①

Hold the pack with the faces towards you and use your left thumb to push off the seven cards into your right hand, then place the rest of the pack on the table. Carefully spread out the cards to show the four Aces, the threes being hidden behind the Ace at the rear of the fan (see illustration 2 below).

Three threes hidden behind this Ace

②

Close the fan, turn it over and then deal three cards onto the table. The remaining cards must be held together in your left hand as the audience believe this to be only one card which you then lift to show is A♠, and put into the card box.

Pick up the pack, face down, in your left hand, then take one of the cards from the table and push it, face down, into the pack. To do this, pick up the card and hold it in your right hand with the right thumb on the back of the card and the fingers covering the top third of the face, so that only the centre pip is visible (as with an Ace). The card can now be pushed a third of the way into the pack and the face can be 'accidentally' shown for a second (see illustration 3 overleaf) as you push the card all the way into the pack. Do not be over-dramatic here: the idea is to appear natural at all times. Now do the same with the remaining two 'Aces'.

Wave your hands over the pack in a mysterious manner and then spread the cards face up across the table. The Aces are nowhere to be seen. Ask a spectator to open the card box, which has been in full view throughout, and tip out the three Aces that have magically joined A♠ there.

③

Tray-ed Secret

Two cards are chosen, each by a different spectator, and are then returned to the pack. The first card is made to fly out of the pack by the performer, while a metal tray is penetrated by the second chosen card.

Type	Location
Skill level	Advanced
Special techniques	None
Equipment	Pack of cards, tin tray

Performance

Ask two spectators each to take a card and then to show the cards to the audience. Lift off about half of the pack to have both the cards returned, then drop the top half back on top of the selected cards, at the same time inserting the little finger of your left hand into the pack above the chosen cards (see illustration 1 below).

①

Break is not visible to the audience

Performer's view

Talk casually for a while and then cut the pack by using your right hand to lift off the cards above your left little finger, and put them to the bottom of the pack. This action means that you have secretly moved the chosen cards to the top of the pack.

Keep the pack in your left hand, as you pick up the tray with your right hand. Hold the tray over your left hand for a moment as you look for a suitable place to put the tray down. As soon as the tray shields your left hand from the audience, push the top card forward, and hold it against the tray with the fingers of your right hand (see illustration 2 below).

②

Immediately, bring the tray, along with the concealed card, away from your left hand. This movement should take just a moment so that later the audience will have no recollection of the pack ever being out of sight. Drop the tray (and the hidden card) on the floor or table as you 'explain' that this particular trick will only work on metal (or whatever excuse you can think of for using the tray).

Now secretly push the top card of the pack about a centimetre to the right as you transfer the pack from your left hand to your right hand. Drop the pack onto the tray and the top card will spin face up as the pack falls, revealing one of the chosen cards. You may have to practise this to get it right.

Pick up the pack and drop it again, but this time the second chosen card does not appear. You try one more time, without success, and you admit defeat. Then you pick up the cards and the tray and the second chosen card is seen to have travelled through the metal!

Tips
This trick is doubly effective in someone else's house when the tray and the cards can be borrowed. If a tray is not available, a thin book will do equally well.

Triple Teaser

The name of a card is written on a piece of paper by the performer, and this is then folded and left in full view. Two spectators are each asked to call out a number between one and ten, and two piles containing the appropriate numbers of cards are then dealt out. The cards are then replaced on top of the pack, and the number of cards chosen by the first spectator is dealt out, to reveal a card of the same value as that chosen by the second spectator. Having dealt the cards again, a card of the same value as that chosen by the first spectator is revealed. The two numbers are then added together and that number of cards is dealt. The last card is shown to the audience and the name of the card written on the prediction is read out: they are one and the same!

Type	Mind-reading
Skill level	Moderate
Special techniques	None
Equipment	Pack of cards, pencil, piece of paper

Preparation
Take two groups of ten cards, from Ace to ten, from the pack (the suits do not matter). Arrange one group so that it runs in sequence from ten to Ace and place this group on top of the pack. Arrange the second set of ten cards to run from Ace to ten and put them on top of the pack. Then put a picture card (J♥, for example) on top of the pack, so that the order from the top down is: J♥, A, 2, 3, 4, 5, 6, 7, 8, 9, 10, 10, 9, 8, 7, 6, 5, 4, 3, 2, A. Replace the pack in its box.

Performance
On the piece of paper, write 'Jack of Hearts' (or whatever card you have placed at the top of the pack). Then fold the piece of paper, so that no one can see what you have written, and leave it on the table.

Take the pack from its box and ask a spectator to call out any number from one to ten; then ask a second spectator to call out a different number between one and ten. Let us assume that the first spectator says 'six' and the second spectator chooses 'eight'. You then deal six cards, face down, in one pile on the table and then deal out eight cards to form a second pile.

Tell the audience that the number of cards in each pile is the same as the numbers chosen by the two spectators. Then pick up the larger of the two piles, place it on top of the smaller pile and then put all the cards back on top of the pack. Say to the two spectators 'You probably do not realize it, but fate caused you to pick those two numbers. I will show you what I mean.' Ask the first spectator to confirm the number he chose (in this case, six) and then deal that number of cards, face down, turning the last card face up – its value is the same as the number chosen by the second spectator (in this case, eight). Put the dealt cards back on top of the pack and then deal out the number of cards (eight) specified by the second spectator. The eighth card turned over has the same value as the number chosen by the first spectator (six).

Then put the dealt cards back on top of the pack, as you say 'The first gentleman chose the number six and the second gentleman chose eight. Six and eight is 14.' Then count down to the 14th card (or whatever card represents the sum of the two numbers chosen by your two spectators) and show the card to the audience. Ask another spectator to read out your prediction, which has been in full view throughout the trick, and it is seen to be correct!

Tri-umphant

Three cards are freely chosen, each by a different spectator, and are returned to the pack at positions chosen by the spectators. Three cards are then taken from the pack, and placed, face down, on the table, by the performer. When the three cards are turned face up, they are seen to be the three cards chosen by the spectators.

Type	Location
Skill level	Moderate
Special techniques	None
Equipment	Pack of cards

Preparation
Put the four Kings on the top of the pack and the four Queens on the bottom of the pack, and replace the pack in its box.

Performance
Take the pack from its box and spread the cards out, face down, on the table. Invite three spectators each to take one card from the centre of the spread and to show it to the rest of the audience, without allowing you to see it. As the chosen cards are being shown to the audience, gather the pack back together and deal it out into four piles.

Ask the first spectator to place his card face down on any of the four piles and then pick up any one of the other piles and place it on top of his card. Then ask the next spectator to do the same – place his chosen card face down on any of the three piles and put any other pile on top. Finally, the third spectator puts his card on top of one of the two remaining piles, and puts the other pile on top.

It is obvious that the three chosen cards are lost somewhere in the pack and, to make the feat look even more impressive, you then pick up the pack and cut it several times. Next you fan the cards, face up, between your hands and look for the King/Queen pairs. Between three of the pairs there will be one of the selected cards which you take from the pack and place face down on the table.

Ask the spectators for the names of the cards they chose and then turn over the cards placed on the table to show that you have succeeded in locating them.

Tips
Instead of just cutting the cards in the normal way, you could use a triple false cut (see pxviii) to reinforce the suggestion that the cards really are well mixed.

Twin Turnover

One card is taken, by both a spectator and the performer and both cards are pushed, face down, into the pack. However, when the cards are spread on the table, both cards have turned face up.

Type	Location
Skill level	Easy
Special techniques	None
Equipment	Pack of cards

Performance
Ask a spectator to shuffle the cards and divide the pack into two. Then ask him to keep one half of the pack and to give the other half to you. Tell the audience that you are both going to turn your backs to them, remove one card, and then turn back round and place the chosen card, face down, on the table.

While your back is turned to the audience, you take one card from your half of the pack, remember it, and then put it, face up, on the bottom of the pack. You then take out a random card which you later place, face down, on the table. (You do not need to know the identity of this card.) You also turn your whole half-pack of cards over before turning round to face everyone. Although it looks as if you are holding your half-pack face down in your left hand, in fact only one card is face down, and all the rest are face up.

Now take the spectator's card and push it, face down, into your half of the pack. Then ask the spectator to take your card (the one on the table) and push it face down into his half-pack. As you reach forward to take the spectator's half-pack, your left hand moves slightly to the right and turns over, so that the back of your hand is uppermost and the majority of the cards in your half-pack are now facing the same way as those in the spectator's half-pack. You then place your half of the pack on top of the spectator's half, and then cut the pack a few times.

Ask the spectator for the name of his card and you then say 'Mine was ...' and name the card you reversed when your back was turned. Then spread the cards out on the table, face down, and there will be two cards face up in the pack: the spectator's card and the one you named.

Tips
When you cut the cards after the pack has been reassembled, lift off about three-quarters of the cards for the first cut and about a third of the pack for the second cut to avoid the possibility of cutting to one of the face-up cards by mistake.

Vanish

Two cards are chosen by spectators, and then vanish from the pack. They then make an astonishing reappearance when they are found, face up, in the pack.

Type	Transposition
Skill level	Moderate
Special techniques	None
Equipment	Pack of cards

Performance
Spread the cards, face up, and ask a spectator to name any card in the pack. Move his chosen card, face up, so that it is the top card of the face-up pack. Then do exactly the same with a second spectator, so that both the chosen cards are on top of the face-up pack. Tell the audience that you are going to make the two chosen cards vanish. Turn the pack face down, take it behind your back and say 'Your cards have vanished – you can no longer see them.' Whilst everyone is groaning at this weak joke, you deal off the top four cards, turn them over and put them back, face up, on the top of the pack. Keeping the cards behind your back, you then turn the pack over and move the two chosen cards, still face up, to the bottom of the pack. So, the cards in the pack are now face up, apart from the four face-down cards that are on top of the two chosen cards on the very bottom of the pack.

Bring the pack, still face up, into view and say 'There you are, I've made your chosen cards vanish.' Again, the audience are likely to groan at such a weak trick so you say 'You obviously don't believe me, so I will prove it to you.' You then push a batch of cards off the top of the pack, allowing every card to be seen, then turn them face down and put them to the bottom of the pack. Do the same with another batch of cards and continue doing this until you come to the first face-down card. You then put the pack down on the table, for it seems to the audience that the chosen cards really have disappeared.

However, the audience may believe that all you have done is slip the two cards into your back pocket. You say that you know what they are thinking, then pretend to take the cards from your pocket, but bring forth an empty hand, saying with a smile, 'After all, the cards are invisible!' Then tell the audience that you will make the chosen cards reappear. Mime taking one of the 'invisible' cards from your hand and throw it towards the pack, and then do the same with the second 'invisible' card.

Now spread the pack across the table and the two chosen cards will be face up: what the audience thought was a joke turns out to be rather a clever trick.

What's in a Name?

A card is chosen by a spectator by spelling out his name, letter by letter, with cards taken from the top of the pack. The chosen card is then buried in the pack but is found by the performer as he, in turn, spells out his own name.

Type	Location
Skill level	Moderate
Special techniques	None
Equipment	Pack of cards containing a short card

Preparation
Make a short card (see pxxiv).

Performance
Ask a spectator to shuffle the cards, then take them back from him and cut the short card to the bottom of the pack. Next tell the spectator that he will remove cards from the top of the pack, taking one card for each letter of his first name and surname, and then he will look at and remember the next card. You demonstrate this by spelling out a name (it can be any name but it must have one letter fewer than you have in your own name). Turn over the next card and tell the spectator that he must also look at the next card and that will be his chosen card. Drop the card you have just turned over face down on top of the cards just dealt and then drop the balance of the pack on top of the cards just dealt. Then you hand the pack to the spectator.

The spectator spells out his name, then looks at the next card. He puts it, face down, on top of the cards he has dealt, and then drops the rest of the pack on top. You take the pack and cut it a few times but, on the final cut, you cut the pack to bring the short card to the bottom. You then announce to the audience that you have a magical name. Spell out your own name, one card to each letter, building up suspense, and then turn over the next card. It is the spectator's card!

Tips

Always use the same name for your demonstration spelling as this will save you having to think up one on the spur of the moment. It is immaterial how many letters are in the spectator's name. If you do not know the person, use this fact to add drama to your performance as it underlines the fact that you could not possibly know where the chosen card can be.

You Are Next

A note is inserted into the pack by the performer and then a spectator is invited to choose a card. Even though the pack is mixed, the chosen card is indeed the one predicted by the performer.

Type	Mind-reading
Skill level	Moderate
Special techniques	Complete cut
Equipment	Pack of cards, piece of card, pencil

Performance

Show the piece of card to the audience and, without letting anyone see your actual words, write on it 'You are next.' Ask a spectator to shuffle the pack and hand it back to you. Spread the cards, with their faces towards you, and insert your prediction card behind the tenth card from the face (see illustration overleaf), again without letting anyone see what you have written.

Try to do this in a casual way, so as not to make it obvious that you are positioning the prediction at a specific point in the pack. Square up the pack and place it, face down, on the table. Now ask the spectator to lift off a portion of cards from the top of the pack, saying that the cut-off portion should be less than half of the pack. Ask him to shuffle the cards he holds, memorize the top card of this portion, place the portion on top of the rest of the pack and then to give the whole pack a complete cut (see pxv). Now pick up the pack and cut it at your prediction card (as this card is different to the other cards in the pack, it is easy to cut straight to it – but to make sure you can make it slightly larger than a normal playing card), bringing it (and the section of cards beneath it) to the top of the pack.

Ask the spectator to turn over the top card (your prediction card) and tell him to read out what it says. Then spell out the message, Y-O-U-A-R-E-N-E-X-T, taking one card from the pack for each letter, and stop dealing. Ask the spectator for the name of his card and then turn over the next card, revealing the chosen card.

You Are the Magician

One card is chosen and placed, face down, on the table by the performer. A spectator is invited to become the magician and to identify the performer's card, which he then does – much to his own amazement.

Type	Location
Skill level	Moderate
Special techniques	None
Equipment	Pack of cards

Performance

Hand the pack to a spectator and say 'For this trick you are going to be the magician and I am going to be the spectator, but I don't trust magicians so I want to shuffle the cards first.' Take the pack back from the spectator and give the cards a shuffle. Then say 'I am going to take one card and you, the great magician, will tell me what it is.' Meanwhile, turn the cards so that you can see their faces, take out one card and place it, face down, on the table. What you actually do, however, is look at the two top cards of the pack and take out a card that matches the value of one of those cards and the suit of the other (see illustration 1 below).

① Note two top cards   You choose one of these two

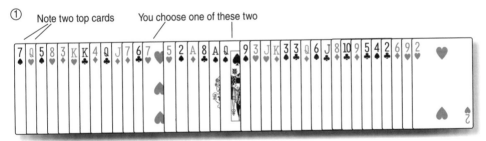

Give the pack back to the spectator and say 'Do you know which card I have taken?' Naturally, the spectator will say 'No.' Then suggest that he deals cards from the top of the pack onto the table, face down, one on top of the other, and say that he can stop dealing whenever he wants.

When the spectator stops dealing, ask him to put the rest of the pack to one side and to look at the pile of cards he has just dealt. Say 'As you stopped dealing at that point, I am certain that you now know the name of my card.' Again, the spectator will say that he has no idea which card you have taken. So you ask him to pick up the cards he has dealt and to deal them out into two, face-down, piles. When he has finished dealing, ask him again for the name of your chosen card. Of course, he still doesn't know, so you offer to help him. Ask him to turn over the

125

top card of one of the piles he has just dealt (let us assume that this is 7♠, as in illustration 2 below), and say 'What does this tell you about my card, apart from the fact that it is not the seven of Spades?'

②

Your card

The spectator will probably have no idea of the significance of this card. So, you then suggest that it might represent the value of your card and you say 'If that is the value of my card, perhaps the top card of the other pile will give you the suit?' Ask him to turn over the top card of the other pile (Q♥ in illustrations 1 and 3) and say 'Now tell me which card I chose.' The spectator will say 'the seven of Hearts' and you then turn your card over, face up, to show (see illustration 3 below) that the spectator has got it right, as you exclaim 'Gosh, how did you do that?'

③

Tips

Sometimes you may find that the two top cards are of the same suit or value, so that you cannot pick a card to match. The easiest way to get around this is to cut the cards casually, making sure that the two new top cards are a suitable pair.

You may also find that some spectators do not immediately see the connection between the top cards of the two piles (ie that one shows the suit and the other the value of your chosen card), so you must be prepared to guide them towards this realization if necessary.

Index

Tricks by Skill Level

Tricks by Trick Type

Chambers & Card Games

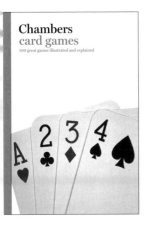

Chambers Card Games

Chambers Card Games is a comprehensive and fun guide to 100 varied card games, suitable for players of all ages and for any occasion. As well as providing detailed instructions, strategies and tips, this fully-illustrated book also features a history of card games and the stories behind the court cards.

Whether you're playing cards alone or with friends and family, for profit or just for pleasure, this book contains everything you need to know for hours of entertainment.

Price: £10.99   *ISBN: 978 0550 10336 9*
Paperback   *420 pages*

Chambers Pocket Card Games

This compact new collection features dozens of great card games, with clear instructions backed up by illustrations, strategies and handy hints, as well as practical information to help novice players get started. From bezique on the beach to patience on the plane, *Chambers Pocket Card Games* is an ideal travel companion as well as a useful home reference.

Price: £5.99   *ISBN: 978 0550 10425 0*
Paperback   *288 pages*

Chambers Card Games for Gambling

Whether you're playing for big bucks or just for pennies, *Chambers Card Games for Gambling* teaches you everything you need to know to play and win at cards. From high-stakes Baccarat to family-friendly Red Dog, this new collection includes fun games you can play at home as well as casino games requiring serious skill and a poker face. Detailed instructions for each game are complemented by illustrated examples and strategies for success.

Price: £5.99   *ISBN: 978 0550 10408 3*
Paperback   *176 pages*

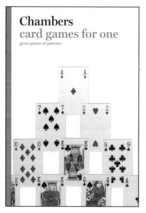

Chambers Card Games For One

Players of all ages and levels of skill will find something to enjoy in this diverse collection of more than 60 patience games. *Chambers Card Games for One* includes classic favourites as well as more unusual games, ranging from easy-to-play Accordion and Clock to the more challenging Flower Garden and Miss Milligan. Perfect for a rainy afternoon or a solo trip.

Price: £5.99   *ISBN: 978 0550 10407 6*
Paperback   *176 pages*

Visit www.chambers.co.uk for further details, or call
0131 556 5929 for a Chambers catalogue.